A Dealmaker's Guide to CFIUS

Answers to Common Questions from Boards, Bankers, and Investors

2019 Edition

Mario Mancuso
Kirkland & Ellis LLP

DEDICATION

This book is dedicated to the public servants of the Committee on Foreign Investment in the United States.

ACKNOWLEDGEMENTS

An enormous thank you goes to Luci Hague, Marina Trad, Natalie Konkel, Olivia Clarke, Olivia Kwok, Ali Krukowski, Aya O'Connor, Matt O'Hare, Kiley Riggio, Ashley Post, Anjuli Das, and Alanna Byrne for their assistance, patience and good humor in the research, preparation, proofreading and production of this manuscript.

Contact Information

mario.mancuso@kirkland.com
(202) 389-5070

AUTHOR BIOGRAPHY

Mario Mancuso, P.C. leads the Firm's International Trade and National Security practice. A former senior member of the President's national security team, Mario provides strategic and legal advice to companies, private equity sponsors, and financial institutions operating or investing across international borders.

Since his return to private practice, Mario has been consistently recognized as a leading international practitioner by *Chambers Global: The World's Leading Lawyers for Business and Chambers USA: America's Leading Lawyers for Business.* Named an "International Trade MVP" by Law 360, he is a leading advisor on M&A and other matters involving the Committee on Foreign Investment in the United States (CFIUS), economic sanctions (OFAC), export controls (ITAR, EAR), and the Foreign Corrupt Practices Act (FCPA), earning praise from boards, CEOs and senior executives for his holistic and "very strategic" approach. Clients say he is "thoughtful, responsive and cuts right to the heart of the issue," and enthusiastically applaud his work as "a highly skilled technician of the law and commercially savvy advisor."

During his tenure as Under Secretary of Commerce for Industry and Security, Mario was the lead U.S. official with immediate policy responsibility for matters involving U.S. industry and national security. As Under Secretary, he served as a senior CFIUS decision-maker and also participated in National Security Council decisions regarding economic sanctions (OFAC) programs; led the bilateral strategic technology dialogues for the United States, including the U.S.-China High Technology and Strategic Trade Working Group, the U.S.-India High Technology Cooperation Group, and the U.S.-Israel High Technology Forum. Mario's extensive government experience includes:

- U.S. Under Secretary of Commerce, Industry and Security (confirmed unanimously by the U.S. Senate)

- Deputy Assistant Secretary of Defense, Special Operations and Combating Terrorism
- Special Counsel, Office of the U.S. Secretary of Defense
- Board Member, Global Markets Board, U.S. National Intelligence Council
- Board Member, CFIUS Advisory Board, U.S. National Intelligence Council
- U.S. Chair, U.S.-China High Technology and Strategic Trade Working Group
- U.S. Chair, U.S.-India High Technology Cooperation Group
- U.S. Chair, U.S.-Israel High Technology Forum

With his senior government, enforcement, and international experience, he is particularly well-positioned to help clients through crises that involve national security-related regulatory enforcement actions or government investigations by the Office of Foreign Assets Control (OFAC), the Directorate of Defense Trade Controls (DDTC), the Bureau of Industry and Security (BIS), the Financial Crimes Enforcement Network (FinCEN), the Department of Justice (DOJ) and/or the Securities and Exchange Commission (SEC).

Mario has authored many articles and regularly contributes to leading U.S. and international media outlets on the subjects of U.S. national security, international affairs and global business.

Prior to his presidential service, he was in private law practice and served as a forward deployed military officer during combat operations.

Professional Associations

- Chair, Forum on National Security Regulation of Foreign Investment in the United States
- Life Member, Council on Foreign Relations
- Lecturer and Senior Fellow, Yale University, Jackson Institute for Global Affairs
- Advisory Board, New York University Law School, Center on Law and National Security
- Member, Atlantic Council
- Visiting Senior Fellow for International Security, Hudson Institute

ABOUT KIRKLAND & ELLIS' INTERNATIONAL TRADE & NATIONAL SECURITY PRACTICE GROUP

Our International Trade and National Security Practice provides strategic and legal advice to companies, investment funds and financial institutions operating or investing across international borders.

Anchored in Washington, D.C., with a global perspective and on-the-ground presence throughout the U.S., Europe and Asia, our team has decades of combined experience working on matters involving the Committee on Foreign Investment in the United States (CFIUS) and other national security investment clearance regimes, economic sanctions, export controls, anticorruption, anti-boycott, anti-money laundering, and related areas.

We routinely work with our clients across industries and geographies on corporate transactions, compliance and licensing, and investigations matters. Our practice is widely recognized as a leading international advisory practice and is distinguished by the breadth and depth of its approach:

- **First-hand U.S. Government Insight.** Our capabilities reflect the perspectives of former senior U.S. government officials and first-hand familiarity with the shifting policy and political drivers of the U.S. regulatory and enforcement agendas.

- **Global Perspective and Reach.** With work spanning 180+ countries, we have the experience and capacity to deliver timely, effective support on a global basis.

- **Integrated, "One-Stop" Advisory Offering.** We offer in-depth experience with relevant U.S. and EU laws and regulations, providing integrated and holistic advice.

- **Thought Leadership.** We play an active role in participating and shaping the ongoing policy conversation around international trade and national security issues.

INTRODUCTION

Notwithstanding its significant economic benefits, foreign direct investment occupies an uncertain place in the American mind. Since the country's earliest years, it has been declared U.S. policy to encourage foreign direct investment in the United States.[1] This historic policy commitment has been reiterated by Democratic and Republican presidential administrations, including as recently as 2018, when Secretary of State Mike Pompeo told a meeting of international investors, "Bring your investment dollars here. We welcome you."[2]

Yet, despite the rhetorical clarity of this commitment, the United States has also implemented an increasingly rigorous legal regime over the last three decades, as foreign direct investment in the country has grown and the nation's national security profile has rapidly evolved. The Committee on Foreign Investment in the United States ("CFIUS" or the "Committee") administers this national security investment clearance regime under the authority of the President and as codified by Congress[3] Helping corporate boards, bankers, and investors understand how CFIUS works *in practice* is the goal of this book.

CFIUS is an interagency regulatory body empowered to review certain transactions involving a foreign person[4] and a U.S. business to evaluate the impacts of such transactions on U.S. national security. CFIUS has the authority to impose measures to mitigate any national security risk posed by transactions within its jurisdiction, and may even recommend that the President block or unwind such a transaction for national security reasons.

In 2018, amid rising congressional and public skepticism of foreign direct investment, primarily (but not exclusively) in response to increased investment by Chinese companies and investors, Congress passed, and the President signed, the *Foreign Investment Risk Review Modernization Act* ("FIRRMA") to modernize and strengthen CFIUS.[5] FIRRMA reflects the most significant changes to CFIUS in its history, broadening CFIUS' jurisdictional ambit to include non-controlling investments in "critical infrastructure" and "critical technology" companies, as well as companies that collect and store personal identifier information of U.S. citizens. For the first time, certain transactions will trigger a mandatory notification – called a "declaration" – to CFIUS prior to a transaction's closing.[6] The timeline for CFIUS reviews has been extended, and CFIUS will have more resources to investigate and pursue non-notified transactions. At the same time, media headlines of deals abandoned, frustrated, or delayed due to CFIUS concerns have become more common. Nevertheless, most deals that are notified to CFIUS continue to receive clearance, and, in absolute terms, foreign direct investment in the United States continues to rise.

This book aims to provide clear answers to certain frequently asked questions from dealmakers about how to navigate CFIUS, including about:

- CFIUS basics, such as what types of transactions CFIUS reviews and what types of transactions CFIUS may not review;
- how CFIUS evaluates the risk profile of a particular transaction;
- the mechanics of preparing and submitting a CFIUS declaration or filing, including what types of disclosure are necessary from parties to a transaction;
- what occurs during the CFIUS review process; and
- how to think through strategic and tactical considerations in specific transactions.

Importantly, this book is not an academic treatise. It cannot (and does not try to) answer every question that may arise about CFIUS in the deal context. Instead, it aims to shed insight on and spark a thoughtful dialogue among senior business executives about how to effectively navigate CFIUS in the crucible of a transaction.

CONTENTS

Chapter 1: CFIUS Basics

1.1   What is CFIUS?

CFIUS is an interagency regulatory body of the U.S. government empowered to review certain transactions involving a foreign person and any business engaged in interstate commerce of the United States (defined in the CFIUS regulations[7] as a "U.S. business") to evaluate the impact of such transactions on U.S. national security ("Covered Transactions").

CFIUS was originally established by Executive Order 11858 in 1975, in response to congressional concerns regarding a spate of investments into the United States from the Middle East.[6] In 1988, after Fujitsu, a Japanese company, attempted to acquire Fairchild Industries, a U.S. semiconductor manufacturer, the U.S. Congress passed the Exon-Florio Amendment ("EFA"), which codified the President's authority to block acquisitions of U.S. businesses by foreign acquirers that present a U.S. national security risk.

In 2007, CFIUS' authority was strengthened and codified by the Foreign Investment and National Security Act of 2007 ("FINSA"), which was passed after the frustrated attempt by Dubai Ports World to acquire operations at certain U.S. ports in 2006. FINSA generally introduced a more structured review process and provided more detailed guidance to prospective filers with the Committee. Additionally, FINSA established regular congressional reporting responsibilities for the Committee and otherwise enhanced Congress' ability to exercise timely oversight of the Committee's activities.

In November 2017, a bipartisan group of U.S. Members of Congress proposed new legislation to address perceived inadequacies in CFIUS' ability to tackle foreign investment risks.

Following seven public hearings on the CFIUS process and several turns of draft legislation, the final text of reform legislation was agreed (with broad bipartisan support) in late July 2018.

On August 13, 2018, President Trump signed FIRRMA into law as part of the *National Defense Authorization Act of 2019* (the "NDAA"). FIRRMA strengthens and modernizes the process by which CFIUS reviews foreign investments in U.S. businesses. While many key provisions of FIRRMA remain subject to clarification and further refinement in regulations, FIRRMA broadly expands the legal authority and resources of CFIUS and, in many ways, is already having outsized impacts on deal timing and other mechanics.[8]

As of this writing, CFIUS' interagency composition is as follows:

NINE (9) MEMBERS FROM THE EXECUTIVE BRANCH	TWO (2) NON-VOTING MEMBERS	FIVE (5) OBSERVERS FROM THE WHITE HOUSE
• Department of the Treasury (Chair of CFIUS) • Department of Justice • Department of Homeland Security • Department of Commerce • Department of Defense • Department of State • Department of Energy • Office of the U.S. Trade Representative • Office of Science and Technology Policy	• Office of the Director of National Intelligence • Department of Labor	• Office of Management and Budget • Council of Economic Advisers • National Economic Council • National Security Council • Homeland Security Council

Certain other offices may observe and otherwise participate in CFIUS' activities, including:

- the Office of Management and Budget;
- the Council of Economic Advisers;
- the National Economic Council;
- the National Security Council; and
- the Homeland Security Council.[8]

In addition to the named members of CFIUS, the Secretary of the Treasury, as chair of the Committee, may invite representatives of other departments and agencies to participate in the CFIUS review process, as appropriate, and the President may appoint temporary members.[9] By way of example, in connection with the 2016 acquisition of Syngenta AG by China National Chemical Corporation, it was reported that the Department of Agriculture assisted, by invitation, in reviewing the parties' joint voluntary notice to CFIUS.[10]

1.2   How can a CFIUS review impact a transaction?

A CFIUS review can impact a transaction's:

- Feasibility
- Timing
- Certainty
- Costs, financial and otherwise

Each of these elements is explored in further depth elsewhere in this book.

1.3   What types of transactions may CFIUS review?

CFIUS has legal jurisdiction to review "Covered Transactions."[11]

Covered Transactions include, without limitation, the following:

(i)   A Pilot Program Covered Transaction (*see* FAQ 3.1);

(ii)   a transaction which results or could result in control of a U.S. business by a foreign person, including by means of a joint venture;

(iii)   a transaction in which a foreign person conveys its control of a U.S. business to another foreign person;

(iv)   a transaction that results or could result in control by a foreign person of any part of an entity or of assets, if such part of an entity or assets constitutes a U.S. business; and

(v)   a joint venture in which the parties enter into a contractual or other similar arrangement, including an agreement on the establishment of a new entity, but only if one or more of the parties contributes a U.S. business and a foreign person could control that U.S. business by means of the joint venture.[12]

Covered Transactions can include transactions without any U.S.-headquartered parties. For example:

• In 2016, following CFIUS review, President Obama blocked the $752 million acquisition of Aixtron SE ("Aixtron"), a German semiconductor manufacturing firm, by a group of Chinese investors led by Fujian Grand Chip Investment Fund LP. President Obama found that the proposed acquisition would threaten U.S. national security due to the military applications of Aixtron's products, and Aixtron's U.S. business's contributions to the significant body of "knowledge and experience" relating to such military applications.[13]

- In 2013, CNOOC Ltd. ("CNOOC"), a Chinese state-owned petroleum company and Nexen Inc. ("Nexen"), a Canadian oil and gas company, made a joint CFIUS filing in connection with CNOOC's acquisition of Nexen. Nexen reportedly controlled 200 deepwater leases of offshore oilfields in the U.S. Gulf of Mexico, which brought the transaction within CFIUS' jurisdictional ambit.[14]

Financing or lending transactions may be Covered Transactions.

- If the foreign buyer acquires economic or governance rights characteristic of an equity investment (e.g., an interest in the profits of a U.S. business) and such rights are sufficient to confer "control" on the foreign party (e.g., the right to appoint members of the board of directors of the U.S. business), the financing or lending transaction would be a Covered Transaction.[15]

- On the other hand, typical loan covenants that give the foreign person a veto right over certain decisions of the U.S. business do not, by themselves, make the transaction a Covered Transaction *so long as* such covenants do not grant the foreign person economic or governance rights more characteristic of an equity investment.[16]

There is no minimum dollar threshold for a Covered Transaction.

- In 2018, one proposed joint venture notified to CFIUS between Cypress Semiconductor, a California company, and SK hynix system ic Inc. ("SKH"), a South Korean company, involved an investment of only $3.6 million by SKH.[17]

- In 2011, CFIUS reviewed — and opposed — the $2 million proposed acquisition in bankruptcy by Huawei Technologies ("Huawei") of certain intellectual property assets held by 3Leaf Systems ("3Leaf"), a California technology company.[18]

1.4   What are the benefits of making a CFIUS filing?

Unless the transaction is a Pilot Program Covered Transaction and therefore subject to mandatory declaration requirements, a CFIUS filing is technically voluntary. The principal benefit of making a voluntary CFIUS filing and receiving CFIUS clearance for a Covered Transaction is obtaining a permanent "safe harbor" for the transaction from any future legal action by the U.S. government to forcibly alter or unwind the transaction.

There may be other benefits for certain buyers. In a broader sense, making and successfully navigating a CFIUS review may help enhance the regulatory *bona fides* of the foreign buyer, something that could be valuable to periodic buyers of U.S. businesses (e.g., foreign private equity sponsors and strategic acquirers). This is especially true if the buyer expects to engage in future M&A activity that may involve the acquisition of a U.S. business that may present more complex CFIUS questions.

1.5   What types of transactions may CFIUS *not* review?

Transactions that are not Covered Transactions are not subject to review by CFIUS.

These include (but are not limited to) the following:

(i)   a transaction that results in a foreign person holding 10 percent or less of the outstanding voting interest in a U.S. business, but only if the transaction is *solely* for the purpose of a passive investment. The foreign buyer cannot in such circumstances have any other indicia of control, including by holding a board seat. This exception is often referred to as a "safe harbor" that exempts an investment from CFIUS' review, but in practice, it is construed narrowly and, upon full implementation of FIRRMA, will no longer be available for certain investments in "critical technology," "critical infrastructure," or personal data-heavy businesses;

(ii)   a stock or pro rata stock dividend that does not involve a change in control;

(iii)   an acquisition of any part of an entity or of assets that do not constitute a U.S. business (for example, manufacturing facilities in Canada);

(iv)   an acquisition of securities by a person acting as a securities underwriter, in the ordinary course of business and in the process of underwriting; and

(v)   an acquisition pursuant to a condition in a contract of insurance relating to fidelity, surety, or casualty obligations, if the contract was made by an insurer in the ordinary course of business.[19]

The CFIUS regulations also provide that loans and other similar financial arrangements are not considered "transactions," except, as explained in Question 1.3, where a foreign person acquires economic or governance rights in a U.S. business that are more characteristic of an equity investment.[20] Given the inherent regulatory ambiguity raised by certain lending structures, this is an area that requires careful assessment.

1.6   When must parties notify CFIUS of a transaction?

On October 11, 2018, the U.S. Department of the Treasury published an interim rule for a pilot program (the "Pilot Program") to implement certain provisions of FIRRMA. Under the Pilot Program, which went into effect on November 10, 2018, some investments by foreign persons in certain U.S. businesses are subject to mandatory declaration requirements that obligate transaction parties to submit a short-form (~5 pages) notice of the transaction (called a "declaration") to CFIUS in advance of closing. Each party to a transaction within the Pilot Program's jurisdictional ambit that fails to submit a required declaration may be subject to a monetary penalty *up to the value of the transaction.* (Notably, CFIUS has yet to provide guidance on how penalties would be determined.) The Pilot Program represents a fundamental change to the CFIUS process, which has historically been voluntary in all cases.[21]

As of the date of this writing, only certain transactions involving "critical technologies" are subject to mandatory declaration requirements.

The Pilot Program sets forth a two-part test to assess if a mandatory declaration requirement applies to a transaction:

First, the transaction must be a Pilot Program Covered Transaction.

A transaction by a foreign person qualifies as such if:

(i)   The transaction does not confer control on the foreign person, but would afford the foreign person:

- Access to any "material nonpublic technical information" possessed by the Pilot Program U.S. business (which shall not include financial information about the business);

- Membership or observer rights on the board of directors or equivalent governing body of the Pilot Program U.S. business or the right to nominate an individual to a position on the U.S. business' board of directors or equivalent governing body; or

- Any involvement (other than through voting of shares) in substantive decision making of the Pilot Program U.S. business about the use, development, acquisition, or release of critical technology.

or

(ii)   The transaction could result in foreign "control" of the Pilot Program U.S. business.[22]

This latter prong captures traditional control investments in, as well as acquisitions of, U.S. businesses that are "Pilot Program U.S. Businesses."

Second, the U.S. business must qualify as a Pilot Program U.S. business.

The U.S. business that is the recipient of the foreign investment must be one that produces, designs, tests, manufactures, fabricates or develops a critical technology that is:

(i)   Utilized in connection with the U.S. business activity in one or more of 27 specified Pilot Program industries; or

(ii)   Designed by the U.S. business specifically for use in one or more Pilot Program industries.

Mario Mancuso

Pilot Program Industries
Nuclear Electric Power Generation
Petrochemical Manufacturing
Other Basic Inorganic Chemical Manufacturing
Alumina Refining and Primary Aluminum Production
Secondary Smelting and Alloying of Aluminum
Powder Metallurgy Part Manufacturing
Ball and Roller Bearing Manufacturing
Semiconductor Machinery Manufacturing
Optical Instrument and Lens Manufacturing
Turbine and Turbine Generator Set Units Manufacturing
Electronic Computer Manufacturing
Computer Storage Device Manufacturing
Telephone Apparatus Manufacturing
Radio and Television Broadcasting and Wireless Communications Equipment Manufacturing
Semiconductor and Related Device Manufacturing
Search, Detection, Navigation, Guidance, Aeronautical, and Nautical System and Instrument Manufacturing
Power, Distribution, and Specialty Transformer Manufacturing
Storage Battery Manufacturing
Primary Battery Manufacturing
Aircraft Manufacturing
Aircraft Engine and Engine Parts Manufacturing
Guided Missile and Space Vehicle Manufacturing
Guided Missile and Space Vehicle Propulsion Unit and Propulsion Unit Parts Manufacturing
Other Guided Missile and Space Vehicle Parts and Auxiliary Equipment Manufacturing
Military Armored Vehicle, Tank, and Tank Component Manufacturing
Research and Development in Nanotechnology
Research and Development in Biotechnology (except Nanobiotechnology)

1.7 What are the potential consequences of not making a CFIUS filing for a transaction that is outside of the scope of the Pilot Program?

The CFIUS review process is currently technically voluntary for any transaction that is outside of the scope of the Pilot Program.[23] However, the consequences of failing to file a voluntary notice for a transaction that is within CFIUS' jurisdictional ambit may be significant. These consequences, and their significance to one or more transaction parties and other interested parties (e.g., lenders, limited partners, co-investors), can vary. This is an area where buyers and sellers will want to consider their position across a variety of scenarios, including, for example, the buyer's plans for expanding the U.S. business, the extent to which the seller may participate in management of the business after closing, and any plans to take the target company public.

Therefore, in transactions where enhanced indicia of national security risks are otherwise present (as discussed in Question 2.2), or in certain particularly sensitive industries (as discussed in Question 2.4), a CFIUS filing is effectively required (while still formally voluntary).

Importantly, CFIUS, with support from the U.S. intelligence community, actively monitors public and other sources regarding a wide range of transactions and commercial activity. This monitoring is increasing in scope and sophistication. By way of example, a Government Accountability Office report released in March 2018 made clear that Committee member agencies actively monitor transactions that could be subject to CFIUS' jurisdiction, but are not notified to CFIUS. In fact, the Department of Defense identified and assessed over 2,600 such transactions in 2016.[24] Moreover, several other member agencies indicated that they would like to have additional resources to assess and, potentially, make inquiries into such transactions.

If a non-notified transaction is of sufficient interest to CFIUS, the Committee may independently request that the parties submit a voluntary notice of the transaction.[25] At this point, CFIUS has already effectively decided that the transaction raises national security questions, and the parties are in a much less favorable position *vis-à-vis* CFIUS than they would have been had they filed proactively.

If the parties decline the invitation to submit a "voluntary" submission, or if CFIUS otherwise desires to commence a review of a transaction immediately, CFIUS has the authority to initiate a review of a transaction on its own. This type of filing is called an "agency notice," in that a member agency may itself submit a notice to CFIUS which is deemed accepted (i.e., CFIUS' review starts) upon the Staff Chairperson's receipt of the notice.

This authority is not hypothetical. CFIUS has pursued certain non-notified transactions with vigor in recent years, sometimes years after closing.

1.8   What is "control" under the CFIUS regulations?

Control for CFIUS purposes is defined in functional terms,[26] and is much broader than how "control" is typically construed by business executives (and corporate lawyers). There is no clear "blackline" test for control (e.g., a specified percentage of ownership or number of board seats). Instead, the Committee considers all relevant factors about the transaction in light of their potential impact on a foreign person's ability to "determine, direct, or decide important matters affecting an entity."[27]

Specifically, the CFIUS regulations define control as the "power, direct or indirect, whether or not exercised, through the ownership of a majority or a dominant minority of the total outstanding voting interest in an entity, board representation, proxy voting, a special share, contractual arrangements, formal or informal arrangements to act in concert, or other means, to determine, direct, or decide important matters affecting an entity; in particular, but without limitation, to determine, direct, take, reach, or cause decisions" regarding important matters affecting an entity.[28]

These matters include (but are not limited to) the following:

(i)　the sale, lease, mortgage, pledge, or transfer of the assets of the entity;

(ii)　the reorganization, merger, or dissolution of the entity;

(iii)　the closing, relocation, or substantial alteration of the entity's production, operational, or R&D facilities;

(iv)　major expenditures or investments, issuances of equity or debt, or dividend payments by the entity;

(v)　the choice of new business lines or ventures by the entity;

(vi)　the entry into, termination, or non-fulfillment by the entity of significant contracts;

(vii)　the policies or procedures of the entity governing the treatment of non-public, proprietary information;

(viii)　the appointment or dismissal of officers or senior managers;

(ix)　the appointment or dismissal of employees with access to sensitive technology or classified information; or

(x)　the amendment of the organizational documents of the entity when related to important matters affecting an entity.[29]

Control need not be exercised.

If a foreign buyer has the de facto or legal ability to exercise control over a U.S. business at the time the transaction is complete, then that person cannot avoid a determination that control exists for CFIUS purposes by voluntarily forgoing, or delaying, the exercise of control.[30]

Control need not be exclusive.

While counterintuitive, under the CFIUS regulations, more than one person or entity may exercise control over another entity. The only place in the CFIUS regulations where there is clear guidance as to a set of circumstances where control is not present is where a foreign buyer would hold less than 10 percent of the voting interest in a U.S. business and the transaction is solely for the purpose of passive investment.[31]

In practice, this "10 percent or less" exception is construed narrowly. For example, acquisition of a voting interest of 9 percent accompanied by a board seat (or, potentially, fulsome board-like rights) could create an argument that "control" exists for CFIUS purposes.

1.9   What is a "U.S. business"?

A U.S. business is defined as any entity, regardless of the nationality of the persons who control it, that is engaged in interstate commerce in the United States, but (under the current CFIUS regulations) only to the extent of its activities in interstate commerce.[32]

This term is broad. Importantly, a U.S. business may be composed of assets with "no distinct legal personality."[33] For example, if a foreign person acquires "an empty warehouse facility" in the United States as well as "the personnel, customer list, equipment, and inventory management software used to operate the facility," the combined assets would constitute a U.S. business.[34]

1.10   What or who is a "foreign person"?

The CFIUS regulations broadly define a "foreign person" as:

(i)   any foreign national, foreign government, or foreign entity; or

(ii)   any entity over which control is exercised or exercisable by a foreign national, foreign government, or foreign entity.[35]

The term "foreign national" means any individual other than a U.S. citizen or person who "owes permanent allegiance to the United States" (i.e., a lawful permanent resident).[36]

The term "foreign entity" includes any branch, partnership, group, association, estate, trust, corporation or division of a corporation, or organization organized under the laws of a foreign state if either its principal place of business is outside the United States or its equity securities are primarily traded on one or more foreign exchanges.[37] However, if such entity can demonstrate that U.S. nationals own a majority of its equity interests, then that entity is not considered a foreign entity for CFIUS purposes.[38]

Importantly, if an acquirer is organized under the laws of a foreign state and is owned and controlled by a foreign national, and it engages in interstate commerce in the United States through a U.S. branch or subsidiary, both the acquirer and its U.S. branch or subsidiary are considered foreign persons for CFIUS purposes.[39]

1.11   Can a U.S.-based private equity fund with foreign investors or limited partners be considered a "foreign person"?

In some circumstances, yes.[40] On this point in particular, CFIUS agency practice is evolving rapidly, and will change further when certain provisions relating to investment funds in FIRRMA become effective through implementing regulations.

U.S.-domiciled private equity funds may be considered foreign persons (and control transactions involving such funds could be subject to review under CFIUS) if a foreign person (for example, a dominant limited partner) has the power or the authority to determine, direct, or decide important matters affecting the private equity fund.[41]

The fund should, at a minimum, ensure that CFIUS counsel evaluate the limited partner base of the investing fund, the owner- ship of the manager/general partner, and other relevant details. For these purposes, if there are different funds of a private equity sponsor investing in a transaction, CFIUS will aggregate a limited partner's stakes across funds *and* consider whether a limited part- ner is also co-investing alongside the sponsor's acquisition vehicle.

The decision whether, and to what extent, to accept foreign limited partners or co-investors should be carefully considered in light of the fund's desired investment universe, especially if the fund may invest in businesses that are especially sensitive for CFIUS purposes (see Question 2.4).

In addition, as anchor investors in private equity funds frequently negotiate for ownership interests in the general partner or man- agement company, including in return for a sizeable investment in the sponsor's fund(s), general and limited partners should take note of whether such arrangements may, in due course, raise CFIUS concerns where the anchor investor is a foreign person — especially if the anchor investor has formal or informal relation- ships with a foreign government. Specifically, if a foreign owner owns a non-trivial, CFIUS control-style stake in a general partner or management company, CFIUS may deem fund vehicles — and portfolio companies owned by the fund — to be "foreign persons" within the meaning of the CFIUS regulations.

1.12 How does CFIUS view foreign government-affiliated investors?[42]

CFIUS is particularly interested in reviewing transactions involving foreign acquirers (whether as primary parties to a transaction, co-investors or, in many cases, limited partners) with ties to a foreign government,[43] and often requests additional disclosure about such investors. Indeed, FIRRMA provides that acquisitions by foreign persons in which state-owned investors own a "substantial interest" of a "substantial interest" in certain U.S. businesses will be subject to mandatory notification requirements.

Under the current CFIUS regulations, transactions considered to be "foreign government-controlled" are subject to a mandatory 45-day investigation phase after the initial 30-day review period, absent a waiver from the Department of the Treasury.[44]

By definition, a foreign government-controlled transaction is "any covered transaction that could result in control of a U.S. business by a foreign government or a person controlled by or acting on behalf of a foreign government."[45] Transactions that result in control of a U.S. business by, for example, government pension funds, foreign government agencies, state-owned enterprises, and sovereign wealth funds may all be considered foreign government-controlled transactions.[46] Notably, there are no particular rules that apply to sovereign wealth funds in this context; such entities are typically viewed by CFIUS the same way as any other foreign government-controlled entity.

> As a class, sovereign wealth funds are considered "foreign government-controlled." However, for CFIUS, not all sovereign wealth funds are created equal.

In determining whether a transaction involving a foreign government-controlled investor would result in control of a U.S. business by a foreign government, CFIUS considers, among all other relevant facts and circumstances, the following:

(i)   the extent to which the basic investment management policies of the investor require investment decisions to be based solely on commercial grounds;

(ii) the degree to which the investor's management and investment decisions are exercised independently from the controlling government;

(iii) the degree of transparency and disclosure of the purpose, investment objectives, institutional arrangements, and financial information of the investor; and

(iv) the degree to which the investor complies with applicable regulatory and disclosure requirements of the countries in which they invest.[47]

> ## Key stakeholders have recently called for greater CFIUS scrutiny of foreign investors with formal or informal government connections.

- In April 2018, in a statement before the U.S. House Energy and Commerce Subcommittee on Digital Commerce and Consumer Protection, the Assistant Secretary of the Treasury for International Markets and Investment Policy indicated that CFIUS is confronting added complexity arising from a number of different factors, including foreign governments' use of investments to meet strategic objectives. The Assistant Secretary's testimony highlighted the potential risks posed by state-backed investors, noting, for example, that acquisitions in technology hardware, technology services or the financial services industry could give such investors access to sensitive information on U.S. citizens that could be exploited to the detriment of U.S. national security.[48]

1.13 Who can make a CFIUS filing? What happens in a hostile transaction?

Typically, all of the transaction parties must cooperate in preparing and filing a joint voluntary notice because the regulations set forth information to be included in the notice that is specific to both the foreign buyer and the U.S. business. Moreover, as a tactical matter, the parties are better able to advocate for clearance of the transaction if they work together to prepare the filing and otherwise coordinate their engagement with CFIUS.

Nevertheless, if one or more of the transaction parties does not participate in the filing of a voluntary notice — due to a hostile transaction or otherwise — then the filing party may file on its own and need only provide information pertaining to the non-cooperating party (e.g., the target company) "to the extent known or reasonably available" to the filing party.[49] CFIUS will then complete its review based on the information otherwise available to it.

While CFIUS has the authority to compel production of relevant documents from parties pursuant to an executive subpoena,[50] the Committee has infrequently needed to exercise this authority.

1.14 What information is publicly available about CFIUS filings and the CFIUS review process?

Any materials submitted to CFIUS, in a pre-filing, filing, or declaration, in connection with the Committee's review process are confidential, not subject to the Freedom of Information Act ("FOIA"), and may not be made public under penalty of law, except under limited circumstances involving administrative or judicial actions or disclosure to domestic or foreign ally governmental entities.[51] However, it is advisable as a matter of agency practice that the transaction parties affirmatively, and in writing, claim confidential treatment for any submissions (including emails) to CFIUS.

CFIUS is known to have an excellent track record for maintaining the confidentiality required by the statute. FINSA, however, authorized limited, non-public disclosures by CFIUS to members of Congress and relevant congressional committees regarding Covered Transactions for which review and/or investigation is complete, or regarding parties' compliance with a mitigation agreement or condition imposed with respect to a transaction.[52] FIRRMA expanded the scope of CFIUS' ability to share information by authorizing disclosure of any information (i) relevant to a judicial action or proceeding or (ii) important to the national security analysis or actions of CFIUS to any domestic governmental entity or any foreign governmental entity of a U.S. ally or partner as directed by the Staff Chairperson.[53] Any disclosures by CFIUS are to be made only to persons with appropriate security clearances and members of Congress (and their staffs) are subject to the limitations on disclosure that are included in the CFIUS regulations.[54]

Because CFIUS filings are confidential and not subject to FOIA, most information about CFIUS trends is generally derived from the unclassified version of the annual report that CFIUS is required by statute to submit to Congress. FIRRMA directs CFIUS to include in each unclassified annual report certain information relating to the timing of CFIUS' reviews of declarations and joint voluntary notices.[55]

CFIUS is also required by law to submit the following information for each classified annual report to Congress relating to Covered Transactions reviewed or investigated during the period covered by the report:

(i)   a list of all notices filed, and all reviews or investigations completed within the relevant period, including basic information regarding parties to each notified transaction, the nature of the U.S. business and the buyer's business, as well as information regarding any notice withdrawals and any decision or action by the President relating to the transaction;

(ii)   data pertaining to filing trends, including the number of filings made, the number of investigations, withdrawals, and decisions or actions by the President;

(iii)   data pertaining to the specific business sectors involved in filings and the countries from which investments have originated;

(iv)   information regarding whether withdrawn notices were later refiled or whether such transactions were abandoned;

(v)   a discussion regarding the types of security arrangements and conditions that CFIUS has imposed to mitigate national security concerns about a transaction, including analysis of the methods that CFIUS is using to monitor compliance with such arrangements and conditions; and

(vi) analysis regarding perceived adverse effects of Covered Transactions on national security or the critical infrastructure of the United States that CFIUS will take into account in the following year.[56]

In addition, the annual report must contain a specific assessment related to foreign direct investment's effects on U.S. critical technologies.[57]

An unclassified version of the annual report that is delivered to Congress has, with the exception of recent years, generally been released to the public in January or February of each year containing information for the year before the prior calendar year, although the release has been delayed in recent years.[58] The unclassified report does not focus on specific transactions, but instead provides general information, on an aggregated basis, about the set of Covered Transactions that were notified to CFIUS during the relevant period and larger industry sector trends over prior years.

Other than the unclassified version of the annual report, any public information about CFIUS filings and reviews most often comes from the parties to a transaction — either because they are public companies with Securities and Exchange Commission ("SEC") or other reporting requirements or find it otherwise helpful to release the information (such as in press releases).

Chapter 2: How CFIUS Assesses a Deal

2.1 How does CFIUS evaluate the risk profile of a particular transaction?

CFIUS is empowered to review Covered Transactions "to determine the effects of the transaction on the national security of the United States."[59] However, neither the statute nor the CFIUS regulations define the term "national security." The lack of definition is intentional; the relevant legislative history makes clear that "[t]he term 'national security' is intended to be interpreted broadly without limitation to particular industries."[60] Moreover, the preamble to the CFIUS regulations states that the Committee assesses national security concerns on a case-by-case basis, which permits the Committee to "address the national security concerns that a particular transaction may raise, rather than identifying certain sectors in which foreign investment is prohibited, restricted, or discouraged."[61]

As a general matter, CFIUS looks to the nature of the U.S. business over which foreign control is being acquired and the nature of the foreign person that acquires control over a U.S. business.[62]

A CFIUS review is holistic. CFIUS does not generally look to a single factor about the transaction when analyzing a transaction. CFIUS has explained that in reviewing a Covered Transaction to determine whether it poses a national security risk, it assesses whether a foreign buyer has the capability or intention to exploit or cause harm and whether the nature of the U.S. business, or its relationship to a weakness or shortcoming in a system, entity, or structure, creates susceptibility that U.S. national security will be impaired.[63]

2.2 What factors does CFIUS use to evaluate national security vulnerability?

While CFIUS' reviews are holistic, the most obvious indicators of national security significance are provided in FINSA (and repeated in the implementing regulations). These include, but are expressly not limited to:

- the potential effects of the transaction on the domestic production needed for projected national defense requirements;
- the potential effects of the transaction on the capacity of domestic industries to meet national defense requirements;
- the potential effects of a foreign person's control of domestic industries and commercial activity on the capacity of the United States to meet the requirements of national security;
- the potential effects of the transaction on U.S. international technological leadership in areas affecting national security;
- the potential national security-related effects on U.S. critical technologies;
- the potential effects on the long-term projection of U.S. requirements for sources of energy and other critical resources;
- the potential national security-related effects of the transaction on U.S. critical infrastructure;
- the potential effects of the transaction on the sales of military goods, equipment, or technology to countries that present concerns related to terrorism, missile proliferation, or chemical, biological, or nuclear weapons proliferation;

- the potential that the transaction presents for transshipment or diversion of technologies with military applications;
- whether the transaction would result in the control of a U.S. business by a foreign government or an entity controlled by or acting on behalf of a foreign government;
- the relevant foreign country's record of adherence to nonproliferation control regimes and record of cooperating with U.S. counterterrorism efforts; and
- any other factors that the Committee finds appropriate in determining whether a transaction poses a national security risk.[64]

Of course, the last item is not, in a strict sense, a factor, but constitutes express guidance to the Committee to consider any particular facts about a transaction that it finds relevant to its national security mandate.

CFIUS examines all relevant facts and circumstances of a transaction in evaluating national security vulnerabilities.

The introductory text of FIRRMA indicated that it was the "sense of Congress" that CFIUS should consider certain additional factors in its reviews of Covered Transactions, including:

(1) whether a Covered Transaction involves a country of special concern that has a demonstrated or declared strategic goal of acquiring a type of critical technology or critical infrastructure that would affect United States leadership in areas related to national security;

(2) the potential national security-related effects of the cumulative control of, or pattern of recent transactions involving, any one type of critical infrastructure, energy asset, critical material, or critical technology by a foreign government or foreign person;

(3) whether any foreign person engaging in a Covered Transaction with a United States business has a history of complying with United States laws and regulations;

(4) the control of United States industries and commercial activity by foreign persons as it affects the capability and capacity of the United States to meet the requirements of national security, including the availability of human resources, products, technology, materials, and other supplies and services, and in considering "the availability of human resources", CFIUS should construe that term to include potential losses of such availability resulting from reductions in the employment of United States persons whose knowledge or skills are critical to national security, including the continued production in the United States of items that are likely to be acquired by the Department of Defense or other Federal departments or agencies for the advancement of the national security of the United States;

(5) the extent to which a Covered Transaction is likely to expose, either directly or indirectly, personally identifiable information, genetic information, or other sensitive data of United States citizens to access by a foreign government or foreign person that may exploit that information in a manner that threatens national security; and

(6) whether a Covered Transaction is likely to have the effect of exacerbating or creating new cybersecurity vulnerabilities in the United States or is likely to result in a foreign government gaining a significant new capability to engage in malicious cyber-enabled activities against the United States, including such activities designed to affect the outcome of any election for Federal office.[65]

CFIUS will also consider the proximity of the assets being acquired in a given transaction to certain sensitive U.S. government facilities, such as military installations, critical ports, waterways and airspace, regardless of whether the assets that are the subject of the transaction are intrinsically sensitive.

Most importantly, parties should recognize that national security risk vectors evolve. Therefore, it is vital not to apply the regulations mechanically and to seek advice from counsel who is well-versed in national security policy developments and familiar with current CFIUS themes.

2.3   What is "critical infrastructure"?

CFIUS assesses whether a transaction involves critical infrastructure on a case-by-case, facts and circumstances basis.[66] The regulations define critical infrastructure as "a system or asset, whether physical or virtual, so vital to the United States that the incapacity or destruction of the particular system or asset of the entity over which control is acquired pursuant to that Covered Transaction would have a debilitating impact on national security."[67]

CFIUS' views on "critical infrastructure" are informed, in part, by separately published guidance on critical infrastructure provided, from time to time, by the President, Congress, and the Department of Homeland Security. By way of example, 16 sectors were designated as critical infrastructure sectors pursuant to a 2013 Presidential Policy Directive relating to critical infrastructure:

(i)   chemical;

(ii)   commercial facilities;

(iii)   communications;

(iv)   critical manufacturing;

(v)   dams;

(vi)   emergency services;

(vii) energy;

(viii) financial services;

(ix)   food and agriculture;

(x)   government facilities;

(xi)   healthcare and public health;

(xii) information technology;

(xiii) nuclear reactors, materials and waste;

(xiv) transportation systems;

(xv) defense industrial base; and

(xvi) water and wastewater systems.[68]

While the above list is informative, it is illustrative and not comprehensive, and CFIUS agency practice construes "critical infrastructure" very broadly.

At the heart of the critical infrastructure inquiry is whether the *particular* assets of the United States business involved in the Covered Transaction at issue would be so vital to the United States that the incapacity or destruction of such specific assets would impair U.S. national security. In other words, a transaction may involve a U.S. business that operates in a "critical infrastructure sector," but whose assets are not themselves critical infrastructure.

2.4   What are "critical technologies", and in which industry sectors are "critical technologies" most likely present?

"Critical technologies" are goods, technologies, products, or services that are sufficiently sensitive that, in many cases, they require a license for export from the U.S. or re-export from a third country. But, while many "critical technologies" are intrinsically sensitive, technologies need not be intrinsically sensitive to be "critical technologies." And, as of 2018, CFIUS' regulations permit technologies that are too new to have been formally classified for export to be deemed "critical technologies" pursuant to the Export Control Reform Act of 2018 (the "ECRA").[69]

The CFIUS regulations define "critical technologies" as:

(i)   defense articles or defense services covered by the United States Munitions List;

(ii)   items specified on the Commerce Control List of the Export Administration Regulations that are controlled pursuant to multilateral regimes (i.e., for reasons of national security, chemical and biological weapons proliferation, nuclear nonproliferation, or missile technology), as well as those that are controlled for reasons of regional stability or surreptitious listening;

(iii) designed and prepared nuclear equipment, parts and components, materials, software, and technology specified in the Assistance to Foreign Atomic Energy Activities regulations, and nuclear facilities, equipment, and material specified in the Export and Import of Nuclear Equipment and Material regulations;

(iv)   select agents and toxins specified in the Select Agents and Toxins regulations; and

(v)   *"emerging and foundational"* technologies controlled pursuant to the ECRA.[70]

Generally speaking, transactions involving the following sectors have an elevated risk of implicating critical technologies:

(i)   software;

(ii)   aerospace and defense;

(iii)   information technology and cybersecurity;

(iv)   chemicals;

(v)   machinery and equipment;

(vi)   metals and mining; and

(vii)   pharmaceuticals and biotechnology.

This, however, is an illustrative, but not exhaustive, list.

2.5   How common are CFIUS reviews and investigations?

In September 2017, CFIUS released the unclassified version of its annual report for CY 2015, which provided specific, cumulative, and trend data on Covered Transactions reviewed by the Committee in CY 2015.

- 143 notices of Covered Transactions were filed in 2015.[71]

- Notices involving Chinese acquirers constituted the largest single category of all notices filed to CFIUS for the fourth year in a row.

- In 2015, 66 cases (46 percent) went into an incremental investigation phase, an increase of 34 percent from 2014. Ten notices were withdrawn after commencement of an investigation.[72]

- The President did not take action to block or unwind any of the 143 transactions filed to CFIUS in 2015.[73]

- Separate statistics from CFIUS similarly indicated that 172 notices were filed with CFIUS in 2016. Seventy-nine of these notices went into an incremental investigation phase.

- In 2017, CFIUS reviewed 238 transactions.

Global Filing Trends

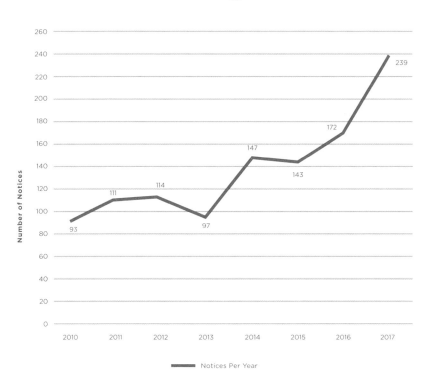

2.6 What sectors and countries does CFIUS review most often?

The CFIUS annual report provides information regarding the particular sectors and countries that are involved in filings with CFIUS during the relevant year covered by the report. As a practical matter, the industry taxonomy that CFIUS uses is somewhat dated and, therefore, not particularly helpful for readers of the annual report to assess current trends.

Subsector Diversity Has Increased

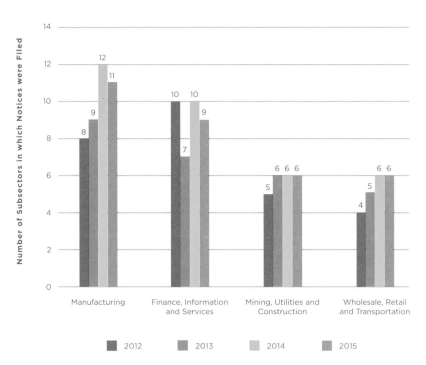

Sectors

Notices of Covered Transactions filed with CFIUS during 2015 involved a wide range of industrial subsectors.[74] Forty-eight percent of the notices were in the manufacturing sector, while just over one-quarter of the notices were in the finance, information and services sector (29 percent).[75] The balance of the notices was in the mining, utilities and construction sector (15 percent) or the wholesale, retail and transportation sector (8 percent).[76]

In recent years, the number of subsectors in which CFIUS notices were filed has increased dramatically, reflecting CFIUS' broadening industry reach.

Countries

Historically, most of the foreign buyers filing notices for Covered Transactions with CFIUS were from Organization for Economic Co-operation and Development (OECD) member countries.[77]

Top Five Countries of Origin for Foreign Buyers — 2015

2015 RANK	COUNTRY	2015 NOTICES FILED	2014 NOTICES FILED
1	China	29	24
2	Canada	22	15
3	United Kingdom	19	21
4	Japan	12	10
5	France	8	6

More recently, CFIUS has been receiving an increasing number of notices from Asian buyers (and China, in particular). Indeed, from 2012–2015, notices from Chinese acquirers constituted the largest single category of all notices filed with CFIUS, which would appear consistent with an eastward shift in global liquidity.

> **Within the past several years, notices from Chinese acquirers have risen sharply, apparently reflecting an eastward shift of global liquidity.**

As an aside, it is important to note that the CFIUS annual report only provides information regarding notices filed with CFIUS for Covered Transactions. It does not describe foreign direct investment generally, as many of these transactions (e.g., licensing arrangements) would not be Covered Transactions within the meaning of the CFIUS regulations. Nor does it cover transactions which would otherwise be Covered Transactions, but for which no notice was filed with CFIUS.

Chinese Buyer Notices

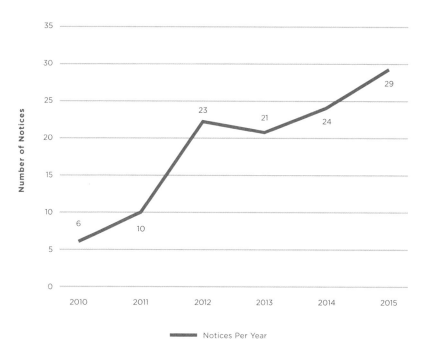

Mario Mancuso

Chapter 3: Preparation and Submission of a CFIUS Declaration or Filing

3.1　What is the process for submitting a declaration to CFIUS of a Pilot Program Covered Transaction?

Like a traditional joint voluntary notice, a declaration of a Pilot Program Covered Transaction requires submission of certain information about both the foreign person and the U.S. business, including:

- Details regarding the structure of the transaction;

- The percentage of voting interest acquired;

- The percentage of economic interest acquired;

- The total transaction value;

- The expected closing date;

- A description of the transaction;

- A summary of the business activities of the Pilot Program U.S. business;

- Details regarding the critical technologies produced, designed, tested, manufactured, fabricated, or developed by the Pilot Program U.S. business;

- Certain information regarding government contracts held by the Pilot Program U.S. business;

- Details regarding the business activities of the foreign person and any foreign government affiliations of such foreign person; and

- A statement as to whether the Pilot Program U.S. business, the foreign person, or any parent or subsidiary of the foreign person has been convicted of a crime in any jurisdiction within the past ten years.[78]

The five-page form must be completed and submitted to CFIUS via e-mail. Parties must also provide an organizational chart of the foreign person, all addresses of locations of the Pilot Program U.S. business (including headquarters, facilities, and operating locations), and certifications as to the accuracy of information submitted to CFIUS.[79]

3.2 How long does it take to prepare a CFIUS declaration or filing?

Assuming that the buyer and seller are organized and cooperate effectively in preparing the submission, a CFIUS declaration can typically be prepared in two to three weeks. A CFIUS filing requires more information, but can generally be prepared in three to five weeks. More time may be necessary for more complex transactions (e.g., those involving multiple foreign co-investors from whom disclosure is required).

3.3 What information about a proposed transaction must be included in a voluntary CFIUS filing?

The CFIUS regulations provide clear and specific instructions for the baseline information to be included in a notice. However, whether, what and how to disclose information beyond the statutory minimum is an important advocacy question, which requires some judgment.

A CFIUS filing must contain an overview of the target business and legal aspects of the subject transaction. In particular, a CFIUS filing must set forth "the essentials of the transaction, including a statement of the purpose of the transaction, and its scope," and must indicate the type of transaction, such as a merger, asset purchase, consolidation, purchase of voting interest, or some other arrangement.[80] The description must encompass the entire geographic scope of the transaction, rather than only the U.S. aspects of the transaction.[81]

The filing must also state the transaction's actual or expected completion date, a good faith approximation of the current net value of the acquired interest, and the names of all financial institutions involved as advisors, underwriters, or sources of financing. The documents underlying the transaction, such as the asset or stock purchase agreement, must be attached as an exhibit to the filing, as well as a table of contents for all documents and exhibits submitted.[82] In addition, FIRRMA requires transaction parties to submit any partnership agreements, integration agreements or other side agreements relating to a transaction.[83]

For a transaction that consists of acquiring the assets of a U.S. business, the filing must describe in detail the assets being acquired, including their approximate value.[84] Here, information need only be provided with respect to the assets that are actually part of the transaction, rather than all assets of the U.S. business.[85] For a transaction that involves contribution of a U.S. business to a new joint venture, the filing must include the same types of disclosure as would be required if the foreign person were acquiring the U.S. business directly.[86]

3.4 What information regarding the U.S. business involved in the transaction must be included in the CFIUS filing?

In addition to information concerning the transaction itself, as discussed above, a CFIUS filing must provide certain details and documents concerning the U.S. business that is the subject of the transaction, in order to identify the business and explain the business's operations, market position, and financial status. These details include:

- basic business information (e.g., name, address, and website);[87]
- business activities by the entity and any U.S. subsidiaries that are not excluded from the transaction;

- a description of the product or service categories of the entity;
- an estimate of U.S. market share for each category of business;
- a list of direct competitors for each category of business;[88]
- products or services (including research and development) that the entity provides to third parties for rebranding or for incorporation into new products, and the corresponding names or brands used by these third parties;
- a description and copy of any cyber security plan for the entity to use in protecting against cyber attack;[89]
- information about the entity's business with the U.S. government (for example, U.S. government contracts);
- any products or services in which the U.S. business deals that are subject to U.S. export controls;
- any technology that has military applications (along with a description of the technology);
- any other licenses, permits, or other authorizations issued by a U.S. government agency (along with identifying details);
- any filings or reports related to the transaction that have been made or will be made to other U.S. government agencies prior to closing (e.g., any HSR filing);[90] and
- whether the U.S. business has been a party to any previous CFIUS filings and any mitigation agreements.[91]

In many cases, it can be helpful to provide additional information to CFIUS that provides color for the argument that the transaction does not present "national security considerations."

3.5 What information does the foreign person have to disclose regarding itself and, to the extent applicable, its owners?

In light of the disclosure required, sensitizing foreign acquiring parties (and in the fund context, limited partners holding sufficiently large interests) to the disclosure required should be an important priority, and one that is ideally addressed well in advance of a client making a meaningful investment of time and resources to pursue a transaction that may warrant a CFIUS filing.

As a practical matter, CFIUS requires very detailed information regarding the structure and ownership of foreign acquiring entities. The buyer must trace ultimate beneficial ownership to the highest levels of its corporate structure. In the case of individuals, the CFIUS regulations require the submission of personal identifier information ("PII"), which certain individuals may be reluctant to provide. In many instances, the regulations may require this detailed information from a very large group of individuals, which may cause significant logistical and social challenges.

All foreign buyers are required to disclose basic information, including each buyer's name, nationality (for individuals), country of legal organization (for entities), any U.S. address, any website address, and, for entities, the address of its principal place of business.[92]

For each parent entity of the foreign buyer in the corporate chain, up to and including the ultimate parent entity, the CFIUS filing must include the name, address, and place of organization. For the ultimate parent entity, the filing must also specify all beneficial owners (if the ultimate parent is a private company) or all shareholders holding an interest of greater than 5 percent (if the ultimate parent is a public company).[93] For ultimate owners that are individuals, the buyer must provide such owners' nationalities in lieu of the legal place of organization.

Certain basic "business identifier information" must also be disclosed for each parent entity and for each of its main offices or branches. This information consists of the business's name (including all names by which the business is known or does business), address, phone number, fax number, email address, and any employer identification number or other tax or corporate identification number.[94]

In addition, the notice must provide the name, address, any website address, and the nationality or place of organization of the person that will "ultimately control" the acquired U.S. business.[95] If there are any formal or informal arrangements among foreign persons to "act in concert" regarding the U.S. business, those arrangements must be disclosed and a copy of any related governance documents must be provided.[96] The notice must also specify if the foreign buyer has previously been a party to any filings with CFIUS and any mitigation agreements.[97]

For the foreign buyer, and for each of its parent entities, the filing must disclose certain potentially sensitive PII regarding the entity's board members and officers and other similar individuals. PII must also be disclosed for each individual (i.e., natural person) holding a beneficial ownership interest of 5 percent or more in (i) the foreign acquiring person or (ii) that entity's ultimate parent (but not parent entities). For example, this requirement could include disclosing PII for individual persons who hold limited partnership interests of greater than or equal to 5 percent of a fund investing in the transaction that is the subject of the CFIUS filing. In practice, CFIUS can (and often does) seek information about beneficial holders of interests under 5 percent.

CFIUS requires that these individuals provide curriculum vitae as well as:

- the full name and any other names used by the person;
- business address;
- country and city of residence;
- date and place of birth;
- any U.S. social security number;
- any other national identity number;
- passport information;
- any U.S. visas; and
- disclosure of dates and the nature of certain ranks of military service.

All of this information, other than the curriculum vitae, is deemed PII, and should be included within a document separate from the main notice for privacy reasons.[98]

Finally, a CFIUS notice must include an organizational chart for the acquiring foreign person.[99] The notice must also include a statement of opinion by the filing person regarding whether it is a foreign person, whether it is controlled by a foreign government, and whether the transaction could result in control of a U.S. business by a foreign person — with reasons for the latter opinion, "focusing in particular on any powers (for example, by virtue of a shareholders agreement, contract, statute, or regulation) that the foreign person will have with regard to the U.S. business, and how those powers can or will be exercised."[100]

3.6 What is the threshold of ownership of the foreign buyer requiring disclosure in the CFIUS filing?

The requirement to disclose certain information regarding shareholders in the ultimate parent of the foreign buyer (i.e., name, address, and nationality or place of organization) does not formally apply to any shareholder owning a 5 percent or less interest if the ultimate parent is a public company.[101] No such threshold exists, however, if the ultimate parent is a private company.[102] In such case, the notice must disclose information for all ultimate owners of the ultimate parent company.

However, the requirement to disclose a curriculum vitae and PII for individual owners of the foreign buyer and its ultimate parent does not technically apply to any owner with a beneficial interest of less than 5 percent, regardless of whether the foreign person or its ultimate parent is a public or private company.[103] Nonetheless, CFIUS may (and does in many cases) request information on owners holding interests of less than 5 percent.

An owner as to whom neither of these thresholds applies generally would not need to be disclosed in the notice, except to the extent that the owner falls within a separate disclosure requirement — such as if the owner: (i) were a parent of the foreign person;[104] (ii) would "ultimately control" the U.S. business;[105] (iii) were a foreign person involved in a control agreement;[106] or (iv) would appear on the required organizational chart for the foreign person (which, notably, specifies no threshold and requires disclosure of "the percentage of shares held").[107]

3.7 Does the disclosure required by the foreign buyer change if the foreign person is a public company?

Public and private companies must generally disclose the same information under the CFIUS regulations, except that if the foreign buyer's ultimate parent is a public company, the requirement to list names, addresses, and nationality or places of organization for owners of the ultimate parent does not encompass shareholders with an interest of 5 percent or less.[108] CFIUS will review any existing public disclosure filings for any transaction party, but filing parties may still want to include any such recent information for ease of CFIUS' review. At the very least, parties will want to make sure their disclosure in any CFIUS filing is consistent with any other public disclosure any of the parties has made.

As a tactical matter, private companies will want to consider carefully how best to provide accurate and tactically helpful disclosure to the Committee, since CFIUS does not have the benefit (and/or burden) of reviewing existing public securities-related filings.

3.8   What information does the foreign buyer have to disclose regarding its own business operations and its going-forward plans for the U.S. business?

Generally, the foreign buyer, along with its ultimate parent, must provide:

- an overview of their businesses, including information such as would be contained in an annual report;

- details of the business operations that the foreign person and its parents have with the U.S. government, including any CAGE code;

- NAICS codes and Dun and Bradstreet DUNS numbers for each business; and

- the most recent annual reports of the foreign person, each of its subsidiaries, and its immediate parent.[109] If the financial results of any of these entities are consolidated into a parent entity's annual report, that report may be provided and individual reports for such entities need not be submitted.[110] Generally, the annual reports will be attached as an exhibit to the filing.

Parties can submit a partially redacted copy of the reports or financial statements to ensure that non-public information is not disclosed to counsel for counterparties, if so desired and consistent with the parties' transaction documents.

If the foreign person is "controlled by or acting on behalf of a foreign government, including as an agent or representative, or in some similar capacity," that fact must be disclosed and the foreign government must be identified.[111] A foreign government is any non-U.S. body exercising governmental functions, including national and sub-national governments, departments, agencies, and municipalities.[112]

Going-Forward Plans

A CFIUS filing must specify any plans of the foreign person to make certain changes with respect to the U.S. business, such as:

(i)   scaling back, closing, or divesting any research and development facility;

(ii)   changing product quality;

(iii)   closing any U.S. facility or moving it abroad;

(iv)   consolidating or divesting any product lines or technology;

(v)   modifying or terminating any of the government contracts that are required to be disclosed as part of the CFIUS filing; or

(vi) selling products solely to non-domestic markets.[113]

3.9   What information must be disclosed concerning foreign government involvement in the foreign acquiring person?

As discussed above in Question 1.12, if the foreign buyer is "controlled by or acting on behalf of a foreign government, including as an agent or representative, or in some similar capacity," that fact must be disclosed and the foreign government must be identified within the CFIUS notice.[114]

Parties will want to carefully consider at the outset of any Covered Transaction whether there may be any indication that the foreign buyer is controlled or influenced, directly or indirectly, by law or in fact, a foreign government, in order to properly account for this fact in their assessment of the CFIUS profile of the transaction and in their broader advocacy strategy and tactics. The CFIUS regulations require substantial disclosure regarding the involvement of a foreign government[115] in a Covered Transaction, and members of Congress and industry stakeholders have called for greater scrutiny of investors that are formally or informally affiliated with a foreign government.[116]

3.10   Who certifies a CFIUS filing and what is required in a certification?

Each party to a CFIUS notice must provide an executed certification with the filing, which, as of October 2018, need be provided only as an e-copy.[117] The certification must be executed by the chief executive officer of each party to the transaction, or by another duly authorized designee of each party.[118]

By regulation, a certification attests that a CFIUS filing "fully complies" with the requirements of the CFIUS regulations and any agreements or conditions with CFIUS or any member of CFIUS. A certification further attests that the notice is materially accurate and not misleading, and complete with respect to the transaction and with respect to the party providing the certification, as well as the party's parents, subsidiaries, and related entities as described in the filing.[119] CFIUS publishes a sample certification that parties may use.[120]

In addition, in the event that any party to a notice files additional information during a review or investigation, either pursuant to a request by CFIUS or on its own accord, such party must also submit a new, final certification at the conclusion of the review or investigation phase, as applicable.[121] If a filing is pulled and re-filed, parties must submit new certifications for any subsequent filings.

3.11 What occurs after the parties have submitted a CFIUS notice?

Once the parties have filed a completed CFIUS notice, and the notice is formally "accepted" for review by CFIUS, a Department of the Treasury official designated by the Secretary of the Treasury (the "Staff Chairperson") will circulate the notice to all CFIUS members for review. If a case officer has not been assigned to the filing, the Staff Chairperson will assign a case officer to the matter, and may also designate a lead agency or agencies to spearhead CFIUS' substantive review.[122]

> Not every filing warrants extensive engagement with CFIUS. Deciding when and how to engage with the CFIUS case officer and CFIUS member agencies during a CFIUS review and investigation should be carefully evaluated in light of the circumstances of a particular filing and the U.S. policy context.

The CFIUS Case Officer's Role

The case officer's role is procedurally and substantively critical to the CFIUS review process, as the case officer is responsible for coordinating action items related to that particular filing, including engaging with his or her counterparts at the various member agencies and facilitating the inter-agency review process. While the Department of the Treasury's Office of the General Counsel and other government lawyers play an important role in every CFIUS review, it is important to remember that the CFIUS review is primarily a national security policy (and not legal) review. This has important practical implications, as it effectively requires that outside counsel working with CFIUS understand and appreciate U.S. national security policy concerns in addition to the CFIUS legal regime.

The Lead Agency's Role

In connection with each notice received by CFIUS, the Staff Chairperson may designate, as appropriate, a member or members of the Committee to be the lead agency or agencies on behalf of the Committee. The lead agency is selected based on its particular substantive expertise and knowledge with respect to the

U.S. business implicated in a given transaction. For example, cases involving critical infrastructure are often referred to the Department of Homeland Security, while cases involving defense contractors are generally referred to the Department of Defense. In some cases, more than one lead agency may be designated.

The lead agency or agencies guide the substantive review process, having principal responsibility for all, or a significant portion, of the review or investigation. The lead agency or agencies may negotiate, enter into, monitor and enforce mitigation agreements on behalf of CFIUS,[123] and also plays or play a key role in determining whether a review should proceed to a 45-day investigation. However, the lead agency only acts on behalf of CFIUS; it does not have unilateral decision-making authority for CFIUS as a whole. While the lead agency may be primarily responsible for a particular transaction review, CFIUS' normal procedural rules apply and decisions are made by the Committee as a body.

Chapter 4: What Happens After a CFIUS Filing is Submitted?

4.1   What is the general timeline for a CFIUS filing?

Prior to formally filing a notice, parties may provide a "draft notice" (frequently referred to as a "pre-filing") to CFIUS five days or more before the filing of the formal notice or, less frequently, may arrange an informal consultation with CFIUS.[124] While not required of the parties, and not binding on CFIUS, filing a draft notice provides an opportunity for CFIUS to request that additional information (or clarity) be included in the formal notice.[125] Filing a draft notice may also help to expedite CFIUS' review of the relevant transaction once the formal notice is submitted to CFIUS and accepted for filing. The draft notice is assigned to a case officer who will almost always remain as the primary point of contact for the filing throughout the filing's review and, if applicable, investigation.

After receiving a formal notice submission, CFIUS reviews the submission before accepting it to determine whether any additional information should be submitted.[126] Where parties to a notice have filed a draft notice prior to the filing of the formal notice, the CFIUS case officer can often formally accept the filing more quickly because he or she has already had an opportunity to review the draft notice and assess the legal sufficiency of the draft notice. However, the time taken to formally accept a notice, and thus to commence the regulatory review period, "depends upon a variety of factors, including the notice itself and whether parties have submitted a draft notice before submitting the formal notice,"[127] federal holiday schedules, and CFIUS' workload generally. In certain cases, final filings may be formally accepted by CFIUS within a day or two of submission; in other cases, it may take several weeks or over a month for CFIUS to formally accept a notice submission.

> ## The decision to pre-file or not may have important tactical and deal-planning implications.

Once CFIUS formally accepts the filing, CFIUS must complete its initial review within 45 days.[128] In the event that the parties to a transaction do not make a voluntary filing and CFIUS unilaterally initiates a review of a transaction, CFIUS must complete its initial review within 45 days of initiating the review.[129]

At the end of the initial review period, CFIUS may either clear the transaction or commence an incremental 45-day review phase referred to as the investigation phase. In certain limited circumstances, this investigation is mandatory absent a waiver. If CFIUS notifies the parties that it will be undertaking an investigation of a transaction at the end of the initial review period, CFIUS must complete the investigation within 45 days of the date on which the investigation commenced.[130] Thus, a review followed by an investigation may take as long as 90 days before CFIUS makes a determination with respect to a given transaction. However, if a party withdraws a notice for any reason and then refiles the notice, the CFIUS review process will restart from the beginning.[131]

> ## In some cases, a 45-day investigation phase may be mandatory, absent a waiver.

Parties are able to withdraw and resubmit CFIUS filings, which a party may consider doing for a number of reasons, including significant changes in the terms of a transaction or difficulty meeting the information request deadlines imposed by CFIUS. Therefore, in certain circumstances, the CFIUS review process may take well over 90 days to conclude. Moreover, FIRRMA provides that CFIUS may extend a 45-day investigation by one period of 15 days for "extraordinary circumstances."[132] Approximately 2 percent of the notices submitted in 2015 were withdrawn during the initial 30-day review, and approximately 7 percent of the transactions investigated during that period were withdrawn before a final determination was reached.[133] By contrast, in 2017, at least 15 notices were withdrawn and refiled, at least once, and the number was likely higher in 2018.

If CFIUS refers a transaction to the President for action at the conclusion of the investigation, the President must take action within 15 days of the date of referral.[134] It is rare that a transaction is referred to the President, generally because most transaction parties will abandon a transaction rather than risk a presidential decision (which becomes public).

As a result, once a formal filing is submitted by the parties, it often takes at least two to three months to receive a determination from CFIUS. In complex transactions, it can take considerably longer. This timeline, of course, excludes the time required to gather the facts and necessary documents and prepare the written submission itself, which can add weeks or months to the above notional timetable.

After a CFIUS case is closed, CFIUS may reopen a review of a previously approved transaction only in certain narrow circumstances, such as when a party has made a material misstatement or omission in the initial filing. In determining whether a misstatement or omission is sufficiently material to warrant reopening a review, minor inaccuracies, omissions, or changes relating to financial or commercial factors that do not have a bearing on national security are generally considered insufficient.[135] The Committee's review of a previously approved transaction is subject to the same rules and requirements as those that apply to an initial review of a Covered Transaction.[136]

4.2   What happens during the CFIUS review process?

Upon formal acceptance of the notice, the Staff Chairperson will notify the parties of the date of acceptance and the corresponding start and end dates for the review.[137] In addition, the Staff Chairperson will circulate to all CFIUS committee members any draft pre-filing notice, any formal notice, any agency notice, and any subsequent information provided by the parties. CFIUS will then begin its national security review of the transaction.

Importantly, CFIUS can reject a filing if the notice:

(i)   fails to provide the mandatory contents of a notice;[138]

(ii)   is not accompanied by the required certifications;

(iii)   contains material misstatements or omissions made by a party in connection with a review or investigation;

(iv)   if there is a material change to the transaction; or

(v)   if the parties do not provide requested information within the time period prescribed.[139]

By way of example, a material change to the transaction may include a change in ownership of the general partner of the acquiring foreign person, or a change in the sources of financing for the transaction. Such a change could be grounds for CFIUS to reject the notice and restart the timeline for review of the Covered Transaction.

Once the review is initiated as described above, the Director of National Intelligence will commence a classified analysis of any risks to the national security of the United States posed by the Covered Transaction.[140] By statute, the Director of National Intelligence is required to deliver a report summarizing his or her findings to CFIUS within 30 days of CFIUS' acceptance of the notice.[141] If the proposed transaction includes review by the

Defense Security Service ("DSS"), DSS must submit its assessment of the proposed transaction to CFIUS no later than 21 days after CFIUS' acceptance of the notice. The preparation of these reports and the CFIUS 45-day review process by the relevant member agencies are carried out concurrently, and the sequencing and substance of engagement with these agencies require careful advance planning.

During the initial 45-day review period, parties can expect varying degrees of correspondence and interaction with CFIUS while the notice is being reviewed. In complicated transactions, or transactions where less information is provided, the parties can expect to have a substantial amount of interaction with CFIUS during the review period. In-person meetings with CFIUS are possible, although not always required or advisable.

In other cases that are less complicated, or where CFIUS knows at the outset that the review will need to continue into the 45-day investigation phase, there may be less interaction with CFIUS during the initial 45-day review period. To a certain degree, the amount of time interacting with CFIUS also depends upon how busy CFIUS is during the initial review period. In some instances, CFIUS may not contact the parties at all until they are notified of clearance.

Parties may submit additional information regarding the transaction and must submit certain other information, "including any proposed restructuring of the transaction or any modifications to any agreements in connection with the transaction."[142] CFIUS may (and often does) also specifically request follow-up information from a party, which must be provided to CFIUS within three business days of the request (or within a longer period if requested by the parties and agreed to in writing by CFIUS).[143]

Under certain circumstances where a party is resisting providing requested information, CFIUS may issue an executive subpoena to compel production of information from a party or from any other person.[144] If a party does not provide additional information within three days of CFIUS requesting the information (or a longer time as allowed by CFIUS), this failure can be grounds for CFIUS to retroactively reject a notice that it had already accepted — with the result that a notice would need to be filed again, and the 45-day clock on the initial review period would be reset.[145]

Parties to a Covered Transaction should proactively identify information or documentation that would be difficult to provide to CFIUS within three business days and take measures to address such risks (for example, by translating copies of a limited partnership agreement into English in advance of pre-filing so that the translation may be available without delay).

4.3   When does CFIUS undertake a 45-day investigation?

The Committee is required to undertake an investigation to determine the effects on national security of a Covered Transaction if:

(i)   a member agency of CFIUS advises the Staff Chairperson that it believes that the transaction threatens to impair the national security of the United States and this threat has not been mitigated;

(ii)   the lead agency recommends, and the Committee agrees, that investigation should be undertaken;

(iii) the Covered Transaction is a foreign government-controlled transaction; or

(iv) the Covered Transaction would result in control by a foreign person of critical infrastructure within the United States where such transaction could impair the U.S. national security, and such impairment has not been mitigated, unless the Secretary of the Treasury and the head of any lead agency determine after the review period that the Covered Transaction will not impair the national security of the United States,[146] or the Committee unanimously makes a determination not to undertake an investigation with respect to a particular transaction.[147] Essentially, if a lead agency or chair determines that an investigation is appropriate, there is little the parties can do to avoid one.

Percentage of CFIUS Reviews Proceeding to a 45-Day Investigation

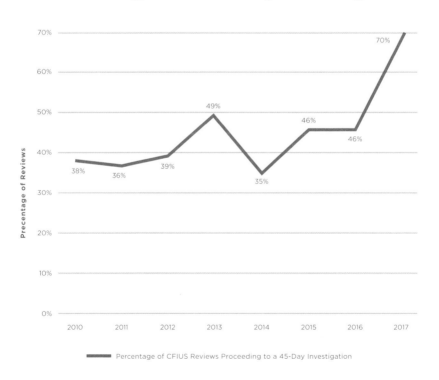

A Covered Transaction may also enter a 45-day investigation if CFIUS is simply unable to complete its review in the initial 45-day review period due to staffing or other resource constraints.

4.4   What happens if CFIUS identifies national security risks in its review?

CFIUS may enter into a mitigation agreement "in order to mitigate any threat to the national security of the United States that arises as a result of the covered transaction."[148] This is a broad grant of authority and CFIUS' ability to choose to enter into a mitigation agreement is not otherwise limited by statute or regulation (except with respect to the substance of mitigation agreements, as discussed below).

Mitigation Measures

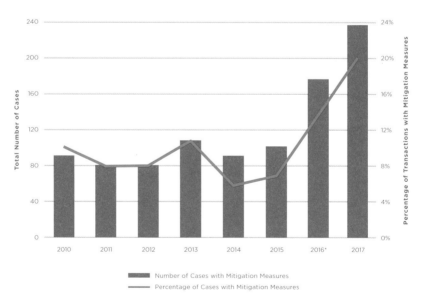

*The percentage of cases for which CFIUS required mitigation measures was not available at the time of this writing.

The lead agency, rather than CFIUS as a whole, may also enter into a mitigation agreement or impose a condition to CFIUS clearance.[149] Depending on the lead agency assigned to review the transaction, parties in transactions with national security circumstances may want to consider during the review process what mitigation measures could be imposed and whether they would be acceptable to the transaction parties.

In 2015, mitigation measures were imposed in connection with 8 percent of Covered Transactions.

Illustrative Mitigation Measures

In 2015, CFIUS imposed mitigation measures requiring foreign buyers to:

- ensure that only authorized persons have access to certain technology and information, and that the foreign buyer not have direct or remote access to systems that hold such information;

- establish a Corporate Security Committee and other mechanisms to ensure compliance with all required actions, including the appointment of a U.S. government-approved security officer or member of the board of directors and requirements for security policies, annual reports, and independent audits;

- establish guidelines and terms for handling existing or future U.S. government contracts, U.S. government customer information, and other sensitive information;

- ensure that only U.S. persons handle certain products and services, and ensuring that certain activities and products are located only in the United States;

- notify security officers or relevant U.S. government parties in advance of foreign national visits to the U.S. business;

- notify relevant U.S. government parties of any awareness of any vulnerability or security incidents;

- provide the U.S. government with the right to review certain business decisions and object if they raise national security concerns;

- notifications to customers regarding the change in ownership;

- exclude certain sensitive assets from the transaction;

- adopt security protocols to ensure the integrity of software or goods sold to the U.S. government; and

- assure continuity of supply for defined periods, and notify and consult before taking certain business decisions with certain rights if the company decides to exit a business line. This measure included establishment of meetings to discuss business plans that might affect U.S. government supply or national security considerations.

4.5 How does the mitigation agreement negotiation process work?

CFIUS may require the parties to sign a mitigation agreement as a condition to approving a transaction.[150] While the agreement is technically voluntary, it is in practice required in order to secure CFIUS clearance.

If CFIUS proposes a mitigation agreement, the parties' options are to:

(i)   negotiate and sign the agreement;

(ii)   refuse the terms of the agreement and withdraw the transaction from CFIUS' consideration; or

(iii)   refuse the terms of the agreement, and let CFIUS make a recommendation to the President that the transaction be blocked.

In practice, CFIUS has significant leverage in the negotiation of mitigation terms. However, such leverage is not infinite, and it is still often possible for the parties to negotiate these agreements. Finally, CFIUS generally does not propose a mitigation agreement until close to the end of the 45-day investigation phase. As a practical matter, parties may only have a few days to consider the terms of the agreement, negotiate where possible, and decide whether they are willing to sign the agreement. If parties need additional time to consider these issues or to engage with CFIUS, they may need to withdraw their notice and refile in order to restart the CFIUS clock.

The capabilities of CFIUS' intelligence function have increased in recent years.

CFIUS regularly monitors and audits companies' compliance with CFIUS mitigation agreements, and CFIUS' capabilities for doing so have improved in recent years.[151] Moreover, FIRRMA prioritizes this by establishing a "CFIUS Fund" which will be funded by Congress in the amount of $20 million annually, and authorizing CFIUS to supplement the CFIUS Fund by assessing a fee for each notified transaction in an amount not to exceed the lesser of 1% of the transaction value or $300,000.[152]

Some mitigation agreements require periodic reporting of certain information related to the company's products, government contracts, and security procedures. CFIUS reviews these reports and regularly engages with parties subject to such reporting requirements. The Committee may also conduct on-site audits of companies subject to mitigation agreements. It is important to note that while CFIUS' main interest is in ensuring proper compliance with mitigation agreements, the violation of an agreement may subject a company to civil penalties and liquidated damages, among other potential penalties.[153]

FIRRMA builds out CFIUS' authority to address noncompliance with mitigation agreements by providing that CFIUS may:

(i) negotiate a plan of action for the party or parties to remediate the lack of compliance, with failure to abide by the plan or otherwise remediate the lack of compliance serving as the basis for the Committee to find a material breach of the agreement or condition;

(ii) require that the party or parties submit a written notice under clause (i) of subsection (b)(1)(C) or a declaration under clause (v) of that subsection with respect to a Covered Transaction initiated after the date of the determination of noncompliance and before the date that is five years after the date of the determination to the Committee to initiate a review of the transaction under subsection (b); or

(iii) seek injunctive relief.[154]

4.6   How is CFIUS action concluded?

A CFIUS review may be concluded in various ways, including:

(i) approval of the transaction by CFIUS after a review or investigation (possibly after execution of a mitigation agreement);

(ii) if the case is referred to the President, either by the President declining to take action or issuing an order to block or unwind the transaction; or

(iii) the parties' withdrawal of the voluntary notice.

In particular, if CFIUS is unable to approve a transaction on its own after a 45-day investigation and decides not to extend the investigation by an additional 15 days, CFIUS will send a report to the President requesting his or her decision. CFIUS may either provide a recommendation that the transaction be blocked, notify the President that CFIUS is unable to determine whether to make such a recommendation, or otherwise request that the President make a *de novo* determination with respect to the Covered Transaction.[155] The President may then take action, or decline to do so.

The President has exercised the authority to unwind or block six transactions in CFIUS' history.

On a procedural level, in order for a review or investigation to be eligible for conclusion, CFIUS will generally direct that the parties submit a final certification several days before CFIUS expects a review or investigation to conclude if the parties have filed additional information subsequent to the original notice.[156] (But, a request for certifications does not preclude CFIUS from asking additional questions of the parties and delaying approval of the transactions.) CFIUS cautions that failure to submit this required certification prior to the expiration of the time for the review or investigation will be grounds for deeming the parties' original notice to have been rejected.[157]

After concluding all action on a filing, CFIUS will formally notify the parties of the outcome by letter.[158] CFIUS must also transmit a certified notice (for a review) or a certified written report (for an investigation) to certain members of Congress.[159]

4.7 What is the relationship between CFIUS and the FOCI, Hart-Scott-Rodino, FCC, and Team Telecom transaction review processes?

The CFIUS process is legally distinct from these other U.S. regulatory processes. However, since these regulatory processes generally take place in the context of certain mergers and acquisitions, they occasionally overlap to some extent. In recent years, the U.S. government has worked to coordinate these other regulatory processes and, in particular, the Department of Defense foreign ownership, control or influence ("FOCI") review process.[160] These review processes, and any foreign investment clearance regimes that may be relevant (e.g., the Investment Canada Act, German investment clearance), should be carefully synchronized to minimize the probability of potential adverse deal impacts.

Chapter 5: Transaction Planning and Strategic Considerations

5.1 How does the prospect of a CFIUS declaration or filing affect commercial dynamics and transaction planning?

The mere prospect of a CFIUS declaration or filing may impact the negotiating position of a foreign bidder *vis-à-vis* a U.S. business, particularly in an auction or other competitive transaction scenario. In competitive deal processes, the ability of U.S. (i.e., non-foreign) bidders to close a transaction with certainty and, frequently, more quickly can make their offers more attractive than even a higher-priced bid from a foreign buyer in transactions that would otherwise recommend a CFIUS filing. On the other hand, U.S. sellers should carefully assess the CFIUS risk profile of a sale, in order that prospective transactions with foreign buyers that offer compelling value not needlessly be turned away by the specter of a CFIUS review. With careful planning, expert counsel can often help foreign buyers mitigate any disadvantage with economic and non-economic modifications to their bid.

A CFIUS filing may also affect overall transaction timing, particularly if CFIUS clearance is a closing condition to a given transaction. CFIUS review may also add certain incremental costs with respect to preparation of the filing and deal financing (e.g., ticking fees for private equity sponsors). Therefore, careful attention should be given to the likely trajectory of a CFIUS review, based on the national security intrinsics of the U.S. business and the foreign buyer's CFIUS risk profile, so that the overall transaction timelines reasonably account for any CFIUS-related timing considerations.

5.2 When should parties evaluate whether a declaration or filing with CFIUS may be necessary or advisable?

Sellers. Initially, the selling party should undertake a high-level national security vulnerability analysis to determine if its U.S. business may be sufficiently sensitive to prompt a foreign buyer to require that a declaration be submitted in connection with the transaction or consider seeking to notify CFIUS of the potential transaction, or to prompt CFIUS' independent review of the sale.

Buyers. A prospective acquirer should evaluate its own CFIUS "threat" profile well before bidding on a U.S. asset. In the case of U.S. private equity funds, such analysis should include evaluation of the general partner and limited partner base, potential co-investors, governance arrangements, ownership of the carry, and other similar considerations. In certain cases, a U.S. private equity sponsor may be subject to mandatory declaration requirements.

These self-assessment processes should be undertaken in close coordination with experienced CFIUS counsel to evaluate the findings, both for the specific transaction as well as collateral considerations (e.g., for buyers, potential future U.S. acquisitions or co-investments; for sellers, reputational considerations).

As the transaction process starts, the specific parties to the transaction must determine if, as a legal matter, the transaction contemplated by the parties is a Covered Transaction. If the transaction is not subject to CFIUS' jurisdiction (under the Pilot Program or otherwise), a CFIUS filing will not be warranted. In the event that the parties determine that a transaction is (or may be) a Covered Transaction, the parties should determine if the transaction would be subject to the Pilot Program's mandatory declaration requirements. The parties should then undertake a national security review of the transaction, considering, *as a starting point*, each of the illustrative national security factors described in FINSA and FIRRMA.

The parties should also carefully consider:

(i)   U.S. foreign policy priorities with respect to the foreign buyer's home country;

(ii) the U.S. business's proximity to military bases, restricted airspace, government buildings, and critical waterways; and

(iii) publicly available information regarding whether foreign buyers of similar U.S. assets have elected to file with CFIUS and, if so, any information regarding the review process (e.g., whether mitigation has been imposed).

A preliminary national security analysis of this nature can typically be undertaken for a potential transaction in a handful of hours by experienced counsel. More generally, the transaction parties should assess the proposed transaction in light of current U.S. national security priorities, challenges, and themes. When the parties determine that national security considerations are or may be present, a CFIUS filing is generally advisable.

Nonetheless, this analysis should not stand alone — it must be conducted with a view to the broader commercial objectives and considerations of the parties. This holistic assessment will drive ultimate decisions with regard to CFIUS including if, how and when to file.

5.3   When, within the deal process, should a CFIUS declaration or filing be made?

A declaration must be filed at least 45 days prior to closing. While a voluntary CFIUS filing can be made at any point during a transaction, including post-closing, buyers ordinarily prefer to make a filing before closing, with closing being subject to CFIUS clearance. This textbook approach gives the foreign buyer the greatest protection. In this scenario, in the event that the transaction is blocked or CFIUS imposes significant mitigation conditions that one or more of the parties is not willing to accept, the parties can decline to move forward with the transaction. But, this is only one approach. The decision whether to attempt to proceed with a transaction in such a case is a judgment call, and should be driven by the particular facts and circumstances of the transaction.

5.4 How can the CFIUS process be addressed in the related transaction documents?

CFIUS considerations can be built into the transaction documents in a number of ways. Increasingly, transactions involving CFIUS include CFIUS-specific deal provisions in a style similar to antitrust provisions (for better and worse). CFIUS terms may be interwoven with antitrust provisions, but it is often preferable to separate the treatment of these distinct legal issues. If the transaction will involve DSS review, CFIUS and DSS provisions should be carefully and holistically drafted to account for timing considerations and desired risk allocation.

Once it is decided that CFIUS will be discussed explicitly in the transaction documents, the parties need to assess whether CFIUS approval should be a condition to closing and, if so, which party will bear the risk associated with CFIUS approval. While CFIUS filings are voluntary and parties can decide to not include CFIUS final approval as a condition to closing, building a CFIUS closing condition into the transaction documents offers certainty that the transaction will not later have to be unwound as part of a difficult divestiture.

Recent transactions have highlighted a variety of ways that the CFIUS filing process can be structured into the transaction documents, including:

- A requirement that the foreign buyer pay a reverse termination fee, if the foreign buyer terminated the agreement because CFIUS did not approve the transaction;

- The right to extend the termination date in certain circum-stances where CFIUS approval was not received;

- Specified mitigation measures that the buyer would be willing to accept, beyond which the buyer could terminate the agreement;

- Designated level of "efforts" covenants to obtain CFIUS approval and a detailed covenant spelling out the parties' responsibilities to cooperate in the filing process;

- A carve-out for the U.S. government-facing portion of the U.S. target's business, and a flexible definition of excluded assets to include assets that have indicia of national security, along with any items identified by CFIUS; and

- A trust structure whereby U.S. citizen designees of the foreign buyer could, with CFIUS approval, hold the capital stock in trust until CFIUS approval was received or the sensitive assets were divested.

5.5 What should the parties do if the deal terms change after a CFIUS filing has been submitted?

Deal terms often change during the pendency of a CFIUS review. By way of example, the foreign buyer may solicit foreign co-investors whose information would need to be added to the filing, or the basic transaction terms may be altered. The CFIUS regulations require that the parties promptly notify CFIUS of any material changes and file an amendment for any material changes during the pendency of a filing.[161]

Additionally, the CFIUS regulations provide that the Committee can reject a filing after initial acceptance if CFIUS becomes aware of information that materially contradicts the filing or there is a material change in the transaction after the submission of a filing.[162]

Importantly, CFIUS approval is specific to the transaction as it is presented to the Committee. Failure to inform CFIUS of material changes to the terms of the deal may render any CFIUS approval decided on the basis of inaccurate or incomplete information a nullity, and may expose the transaction (and persons submitting and certifying to inaccurate information) to legal risk.

Chapter 6: What's Next?

Initial signals from CFIUS suggest an intent to fully implement FIRRMA as quickly as possible.

Three key trends will likely be significant for CFIUS reviews in the coming year:

1. *Transactions involving "critical technologies" will continue to garner greater regulatory and other scrutiny as the U.S. moves forward with imposing new and different controls on "emerging" and "foundational" technologies.*

   On November 19, 2018, the U.S. Department of Commerce, Bureau of Industry and Security ("BIS"), issued an advanced notice of proposed rulemaking initiating the process to regulate exports of "emerging technologies" in areas such as artificial intelligence, biotechnology, navigation and surveillance. The move represents the first step in what could be a marked and meaningful expansion of U.S. export controls and stands to materially impact many types of transactions involving technology companies, including M&A, investments, joint ventures, strategic alliances, and services and licensing arrangements.[163]

2. *National security importance will continue to attach to deals in industries that have not historically been perceived as risky (e.g., healthcare, entertainment, agriculture).*

   • CFIUS' already broad industry reach will likely continue to expand, as the business benefits of CFIUS safe harbor in an uncertain political climate become more apparent to prospective foreign buyers. In this connection, FIRRMA's focus on increasing CFIUS scrutiny of companies that collect large amounts of PII reflects CFIUS' increasing interest in healthcare businesses that may appear, at first blush, wholly benign from a national security perspective.

- On the other hand, sellers will have to carefully think through how to manage competitive dynamics and reputational risks in deals with potential foreign buyers.

"As foreign entities continue their aggressive acquisitions of U.S. food and agriculture companies, it's imperative that these transactions face additional scrutiny."

— Sen. Debbie Stabenow (D-MI) (March 2017)

---

3. *Non-U.S. national security investment clearance regimes will become increasingly relevant for cross-border deals.*

- Within the past several years, other countries (e.g., Australia, Canada, France, Germany, the U.K.) have adopted more stringent foreign investment clearance regimes. In particular, as of the date of this writing, the EU has adopted a regional investment screening framework that centralizes and streamlines foreign investments into the EU, with a focus on reviewing deals in industries perceived as sensitive (e.g., energy, infrastructure, technology).[164]

- The U.S. will seek greater cooperation and information-sharing with its allies on the administration of CFIUS reviews with its analogues in other countries.

- Given rising EU anxiety regarding investment from Chinese buyers, such regimes will likely take on greater importance for cross-border deals.

CFIUS in the M&A Lifecycle

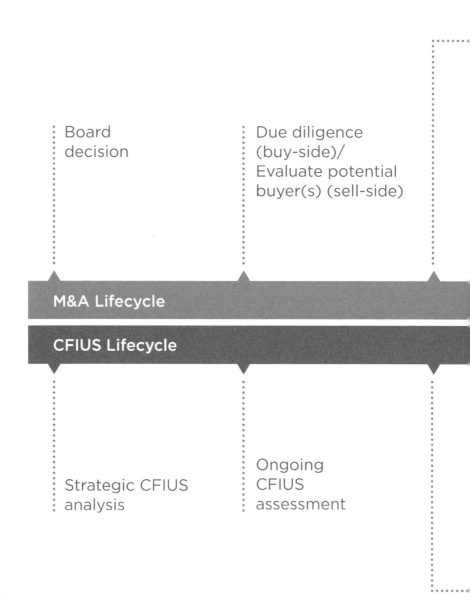

Board
decision

Due diligence
(buy-side)/
Evaluate potential
buyer(s) (sell-side)

M&A Lifecycle

CFIUS Lifecycle

Strategic CFIUS
analysis

Ongoing
CFIUS
assessment

··· Contract negotiation
and exclusivity

Signed
purchase
agreement

Deal approvals
and closing

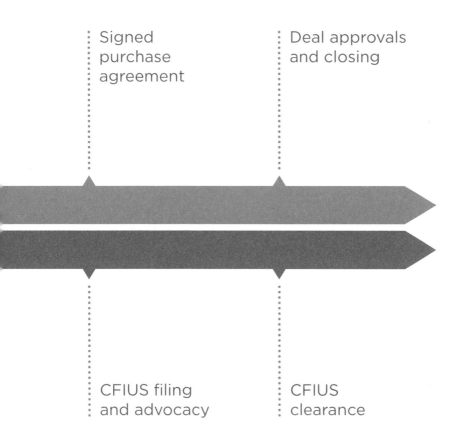

CFIUS filing
and advocacy

CFIUS
clearance

···· Negotiation of CFIUS
provisions and ongoing
CFIUS assessment

Mario Mancuso

Notes

1   In 1782, the United States entered into a treaty of amity and commerce with the Netherlands. Thomas A. Bailey, A Diplomatic History of the American People (New York: Appleton-Century-Crofts, 1958), 40.

2   Mike Pompeo, Remarks by the Secretary of State at the 2018 SelectUSA Investment Summit, Jun. 22, 2018, *available at* https://www.state.gov/secretary/remarks/2018/06/283438.htm.

3   For more on the history of CFIUS, *see* James K. Jackson, "The Committee on Foreign Investment in the United States," CRS Report RL 33388 (Jul. 3, 2018), *available online* https://fas.org/sgp/crs/natsec/RL33388.pdf.

4   We use the term "foreign" to describe "non-U.S." legal or natural persons because this is the term used by CFIUS regulations.

5   *Foreign Investment Risk Review Modernization Act*, 115th Cong., H.R. 5515, Title XVII §§ 1701-1728 ("FIRRMA").

6   See 31 C.F.R. Part 801.

7   Regulations Pertaining to Mergers, Acquisitions, and Takeovers by Foreign Persons, 73 Fed. Reg. 70,702 (Nov. 21, 2008) ("CFIUS Regulations").

8   For additional background on FIRRMA, see M. Mancuso, L. Hague, et al., "CFIUS Reform at the Finish Line," Kirkland and Ellis LLP Alert, Jul. 30, 2018, *available at* https://www.kirkland.com/siteFiles/Publications/CFIUS_Reform_at_the_Finish_Line.pdf.

9   Exec. Order No. 11858, 40 Fed. Reg. 20,263 (May 9, 1975); Jackson, *supra* n.3, at 8.

10 Jacob Bundge, et al., "Powerful U.S. Panel Clears Chinese Takeover of Syngenta," *The Wall Street Journal,* Aug. 23, 2016, *available at* http://www.wsj.com/articles/powerful-u-s-panel-clears-chinese-takeover-of-syngenta-1471914278.

11 CFIUS Regulations, 73 Fed Reg. at 70, 702, 70, 704.

12 31 C.F.R. § 800.301(d).

13 U.S. Dep't of the Treasury, *Statement on the President's Decision Regarding the U.S. Business of Aixtron SE* (Dec. 2, 2016), *available at* https://www.treasury.gov/press-center/press-releases/Pages/jl0679.aspx.

[14] David Gelles, "U.S. Approves $18bn Cnooc Bid for Nexen," *The Financial Times*, Feb. 12, 2013, *available at* http://www.ft.com/cms/s/0/2cc88ec2-7529-11e2-8bc7-00144feabdc0.html#axzz2i1TkjiqZ.

[15] 31 C.F.R. § 800.303.

[16] CFIUS Regulations, 73 Fed. Reg. at 70,710.

[17] *See* Cypress Semiconductor Corp. Form 8-K, Exhibit 2.3, "Joint Venture Agreement," October 23, 2018, *available at* https://www.sec.gov/Archives/edgar/data/791915/000079191519000006/cy-12302018ex23.htm.

[18] Chris V. Nicholson, "The Big Chill: Huawei Imbroglio Puts Countries at Odds," *New York Times*, Feb. 18, 2011, *available at* http://dealbook.nytimes.com/2011/02/18/the-big-chill-huawei-imbroglio-puts-countries-at-odds/.

[19] 31 C.F.R. § 800.302.

[20] 31 C.F.R. § 800.303; CFIUS Regulations, 73 Fed. Reg. at 70,704.

[21] For additional background on the Pilot Program, *see* Kirkland & Ellis LLP Alert, "CFIUS Implements New Pilot Program Requiring Submission of Declarations for Certain Transactions," December 14, 2018, *available at* https://www.kirkland.com/publications/kirkland-alert/2018/12/cfius-implements-new-pilot-program (accessed online Feb. 27, 2019).

[22] 31 C.F.R. 801.210.

[23] CFIUS Regulations, 73 Fed. Reg. at 70,704; 31 C.F.R. § 801.101.

[24] Mario Mancuso, Boyd Greene, and Luci Hague, "This is What the U.S. Government Thinks About CFIUS," *Bloomberg* (April 18 2018), *available at* https://www.kirkland.com/publications/article/2018/04/this-is-what-the-us-government-thinks-about-cfius (last accessed Feb. 27, 2019).

[25] 31 C.F.R. § 800.401(b).

[26] CFIUS Regulations, 73 Fed. Reg. at 70,704.

[27] 31 C.F.R. §§ 800.204(a).

[28] *Id.*

[29] *Id.*

[30] CFIUS Regulations, 73 Fed. Reg. at 70,704.

[31] 31 C.F.R. § 800.223.

32   31 C.F.R. § 800.226.

33   CFIUS Regulations, 73 Fed. Reg. at 70,708.

34   31 C.F.R. § 800.301(c), Example 7.

35   31 C.F.R. § 800.216.

36   31 C.F.R. § 800.215; 31 C.F.R. § 800.227.

37   31 C.F.R. § 800.212.

38   *Id.*

39   31 C.F.R. § 800.226, Example 1.

40   H.R. 5515 at 545.

41   CFIUS will examine whether an investor is wholly or partially owned by, or has other formal or informal connections with, a foreign government.

42   Guidance Concerning the National Security Review Conducted by the Committee on Foreign Investment in the United States, 73 Fed. Reg. at 74,571 (Dec. 8, 2008) ("CFIUS Guidance").

43   31 C.F.R. § 800.503(b).

44   31 C.F.R. § 800.214; CFIUS Guidance, 73 Fed. Reg. at 74,568.

45   CFIUS Guidance, 73 Fed. Reg. at 74,571.

46   CFIUS Guidance, 73 Fed. Reg. at 74,571.

47   *Id.*

48   Heath P. Tarbert, "Statement of Assistant Secretary Heath P. Tarbert Before the U.S. House Energy and Commerce Subcommittee on Digital Commerce and Consumer Protection," U.S. Department of the Treasury, April 26, 2018, *available at* https://home.treasury.gov/index.php/news/press-releases/sm0368.

49   31 C.F.R. § 800.402.

50   31 C.F.R. § 800.701(a); *see also* 50 U.S.C. App. § 2155(a).

51   31 C.F.R. § 800.702(a); 50 U.S.C. § 4565(c)(2).

52   50 U.S.C. § 4565(a).

53   50 U.S.C. § 4565(c)(2).

54   50 U.S.C. § 4565(g).

[55] H.R. 5515 at 563.

[56] 50 U.S.C. § 4565(m)(2).

[57] 50 U.S.C. §4565(m)(3)(A). Specifically, CFIUS must provide Congress with an analysis regarding whether there is "credible evidence of a coordinated strategy" by any specific countries or companies to acquire United States businesses involved in the development or production of U.S. critical technologies, as well as analysis regarding whether CFIUS has any evidence of "industrial espionage activities directed or directly assisted by foreign governments against private United States companies" with the aim of obtaining trade secrets regarding U.S. critical technologies. *Id.*

[58] *See* U.S. Dep't of the Treasury, "Reports and Tables," last updated September 20, 2017, *available at* https://www.treasury.gov/resource-center/international/foreign-investment/pages/cfius-reports.aspx.

[59] 50 U.S.C. § 4565(b)(1)(A)(i).

[60] 134 Cong. Rec. H2118 (Apr. 20, 1988).

[61] CFIUS Regulations, 73 Fed. Reg. at 70,705.

[62] CFIUS Guidance, 73 Fed. Reg. 74,570.

[63] CFIUS Guidance, 73 Fed. Reg. at 74,569-70; *see also* 50 U.S.C. § 4565.

[64] CFIUS Guidance, 73 Fed. Reg. at 74,569-70.

[65] H.R. 5515, 541-542.

[66] 31 C.F.R. § 800.208.

[67] *Id.*

[68] Presidential Policy Directive/PPD-21: Presidential Policy Directive—Critical Infrastructure Security and Resilience (Feb. 12, 2013).

[69] M. Mancuso, et al., "As National Security Concerns Mount, the U.S. Government Announces Proposal to Regulate Emerging Technologies," Kirkland & Ellis LLP Alert (Nov. 28, 2018), *available at* https://www.kirkland.com/publications/kirkland-alert/2018/11/as-national-security-concerns-mount (last visited Mar. 3, 2019) (hereinafter, "ECRA Alert").

[70] 31 C.F.R. § 800.209.

[71] *Annual Report to Congress for 2015, Committee on Foreign Investment in the United States,* September 2017 ("2015 Annual Report").

[72] *Id.*

73 *Id.*

74 *Id.*

75 *Id.*

76 *Id.*

77 Australia, Austria, Belgium, Canada, Chile, Czech Republic, Denmark, Estonia, Finland, France, Germany, Greece, Hungary, Iceland, Ireland, Israel, Italy, Japan, Korea, Latvia, Lithuania, Luxembourg, Mexico, Netherlands, New Zealand, Norway, Poland, Portugal, Slovak Republic, Slovenia, Spain, Sweden, Switzerland, Turkey, United Kingdom, and the United States.

78 *See* Dep't of the Treasury, Declaration Submission Form, *available at* https://home.treasury.gov/system/files/206/Declaration-Submission-Form-for-Critical-Technology-Pilot-Program_0.pdf.

79 31 C.F.R. § 801.402(j)(1); 31 C.F.R. § 801.402(l).

80 31 CFR § 800.402(c)(1)(i)-(ii).

81 31 C.F.R. § 800.402(c)(1)(i)-(vi).

82 31 C.F.R. § 800.402(i); 31 C.F.R. § 800.402(m).

83 50 U.S.C. 4565(b)(1)(C)(iv); 31 C.F.R. § 800.402(c)(1)(x).

84 31 C.F.R. § 800.402(c)(2).

85 *Id.*

86 31 C.F.R. § 800.402(c).

87 31 C.F.R. § 800.402(c)(1)(iv).

88 31 C.F.R. § 800.402(c)(3)(i).

89 31 C.F.R. § 800.402(c)(3)(viii).

90 31 C.F.R. § 800.402(d).

91 31 C.F.R. § 800.402(k)(2).

92 31 C.F.R. § 800.402(c)(1)(iii). For a foreign buyer that is an entity, this requirement is in addition to the requirement to disclose personal identifier information regarding the foreign person's and certain parent entities' board members and owners, as discussed in subsequent paragraphs.

93 31 C.F.R. § 800.402(c)(1)(v).

Mario Mancuso

94 31 C.F.R. § 800.402(c)(6)(vii).

95 31 C.F.R. § 800.402(c)(1)(vi).

96 31 C.F.R. § 800.402(c)(6)(v).

97 31 C.F.R. § 800.402(k)(2).

98 31 C.F.R. § 800.402(c)(6)(vi).

99 31 C.F.R. § 800.402(j). This organizational chart must show all entities or individuals "above" the foreign party "up to the person or persons having ultimate control of that person, including the percentage of shares held by each." *Id.*

100 *Id.*

101 31 C.F.R. § 800.402(c)(1)(v)(C).

102 31 C.F.R. § 800.402(c)(1)(v)(B).

103 31 C.F.R. § 800.402(c)(6)(vi).

104 31 C.F.R. § 800.402(c)(1)(v).

105 31 C.F.R. § 800.402(c)(1)(vi).

106 31 C.F.R. § 800.402(c)(6)(v).

107 31 C.F.R. § 800.402(j).

108 31 C.F.R. § 800.402(c)(1)(v)(B)-(C).

109 31 C.F.R. § 800.402(c)(6)(i).

110 31 C.F.R. § 800.402(g).

111 31 C.F.R. § 800.402(c)(6)(iii).

112 31 C.F.R. § 800.213.

113 31 C.F.R. § 800.402(c)(6)(ii).

114 31 C.F.R. § 800.402(c)(6)(iii).

115 31 C.F.R. § 800.213.

116 M. Mancuso, L. Hague, et al., "Dealmakers, Take Note: GAO to Study CFIUS at Congress' Urging," Kirkland & Ellis LLP Alert (Oct. 17, 2016), *available at* https://p.widencdn.net/jq10mh/Alert_20161017.

117 31 C.F.R. § 800.402(l).

[118] 31 C.F.R. § 800.202(a). For an entity, a designee can be the general partner of a partnership, an officer or director of a corporation, or, if the entity has no officers, directors, or partners, then any individual exercising a similar executive function for the entity. For individuals, the duly authorized designee is the individual or his or her legal representative. In any case, the designee must actually possess authority to make the certification on behalf of the party to the transaction. 31 C.F.R. § 800.202(b)-(c).

[119] 31 C.F.R. § 800.202(a).

[120] CFIUS Res. Ctr., Filing Instructions, Template for Certification to Accompany Notice (last visited Oct. 15, 2013), *available at* https://www.treasury.gov/resource-center/international/foreign-investment/Documents/cert-notice-template.pdf, (hereinafter, "Filing Instructions").

[121] 31 C.F.R. § 800.701(d). CFIUS also publishes a sample final certification, which is materially the same as the sample original certification except for an explicit reference to "additional information" having been provided in connection with the original filing. *See id.*

[122] 31 C.F.R. § 800.502(e).

[123] 31 C.F.R. § 800.218.

[124] 31 C.F.R. § 800.218.

[125] Filing Instructions, *supra* note 120.

[126] *Id.*

[127] CFIUS will refuse to accept a notice if, for example, "the voluntary notice is not complete, the parties do not respond to follow-up information requests within the required time frame, there is a material change in the transaction, or information comes to light that contradicts material information provided in the notice by the parties." *See* CFIUS Process Overview, *available at* https://www.treasury.gov/resource-center/international/foreign-investment/Pages/cfius-overview.aspx (last visited Mar. 3, 2019) (hereinafter, "Process Overview").

[128] CFIUS Res. Ctr., CFIUS FAQs, *available at* https://www.treasury.gov/resource-center/faqs/CFIUS/Pages/default.aspx (last visited Feb. 27, 2019).

[129] 50 U.S.C. § 4565(b)(1)(E).

[130] 50 U.S.C. § 4565(b)(2)(C); 31 C.F.R. § 800.506(a).

[131] *Id.*

[132] 31 C.F.R. § 800.506(e).

[133] 2015 Annual Report.

[134] *See* Process Overview, *supra* note 127.

[135] CFIUS Regulations, 73 Fed. Reg. at 70,715.

[136] *Id.;* 31 C.F.R. § 800.509.

[137] CFIUS Regulations, 73 Fed. Reg. at 70,715.

[138] Filing Instructions, *supra* note 110; *see also* 31 C.F.R. § 800.502(c).

[139] 31 C.F.R. § 800.403(a)(1).

[140] 31 C.F.R. § 800.403(a)(2)-(4).

[141] 50 U.S.C. § 4565(b)(4).

[142] 50 U.S.C. § 4565(b)(5).

[143] Process Overview, *supra* note 127.

[144] 50 U.S.C. App. § 2155(a); 31 C.F.R. § 800.701(a).

[145] 31 C.F.R. § 800.403(a)(3).

[146] 31 C.F.R. § 800.503.

[147] Exec. Order No. 11858, *supra* note 9.

[148] 50 U.S.C. § 4565(l)(1)(A).

[149] 50 U.S.C. § 4565(l)(1)(A).

[150] 50 U.S.C. § 4565(l)(1)(A), (3)(A).

[151] 50 U.S.C. § 4565(l)(3)(A), (B)(ii).

[152] 50 U.S.C. § 4565(p).

[153] 31 C.F.R. § 800.801(b) – (c).

[154] 50 U.S.C. § 4565(l)(6)(D).

[155] Filing Instructions, *supra* note 110; *see also* 31 C.F.R. § 800.701(d).

[156] Filing Instructions, *supra* note 110; *see also* 31 C.F.R. § 800.403(a)(4).

[157] 50 U.S.C. App. § 4565(b)(6); 31 C.F.R. § 800.506(d).

[158] 50 U.S.C. App. § 4565(b)(3).

159 *Id.*

160 50 U.S.C. § 4565(f).

161 National Industrial Security Program, 79 Fed. Reg. 19,467 (Apr. 9, 2014); *see also* DoD Issues Interim Final Rule on Foreign-Owned Contractor Access to Classified Data, 56 Gov't. Contractor ¶ 123 (Apr. 16, 2014).

162 31 C.F.R. § 800.403 (a)(2)(i).

163 31 C.F.R. § 800.403 (a)(2)(ii).

164 *See* ECRA Alert, *supra* note 69.

Mario Mancuso